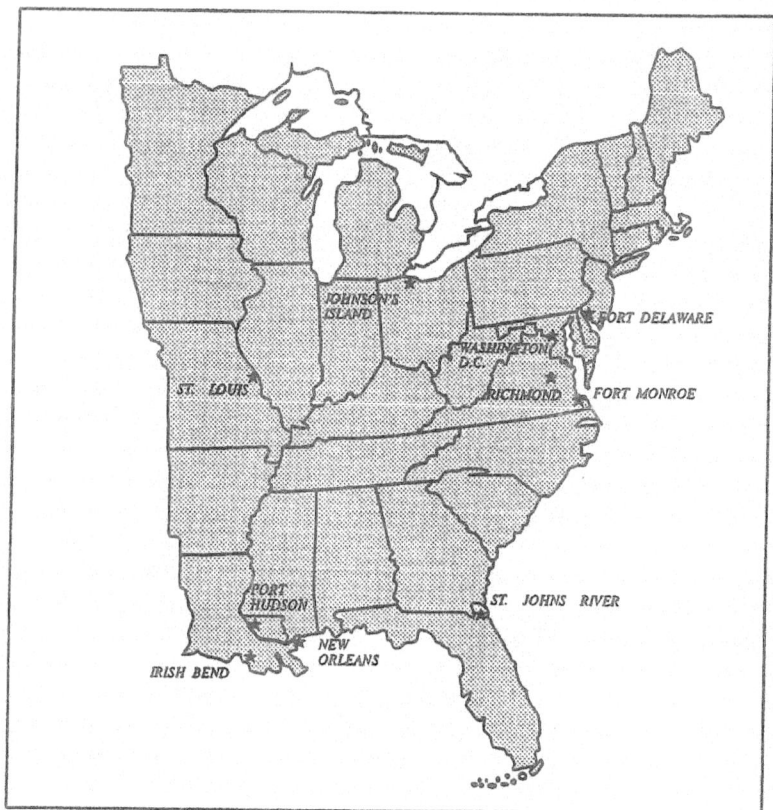

Some of the places mentioned in "Escape from the Maple Leaf"

Escape from the *Maple Leaf*

INCLUDING

A ROSTER OF
CONFEDERATE OFFICERS
ON THE *MAPLE LEAF*

AND

A DISCUSSION OF
THE SYSTEM OF EXCHANGES
AND PAROLES

Col. Jerry V. Witt, U.S.A., Retired

HERITAGE BOOKS
2012

HERITAGE BOOKS
AN IMPRINT OF HERITAGE BOOKS, INC.

Books, CDs, and more—Worldwide

For our listing of thousands of titles see our website
at
www.HeritageBooks.com

Published 2012 by
HERITAGE BOOKS, INC.
Publishing Division
100 Railroad Ave. #104
Westminster, Maryland 21157

Cover drawing of the *Maple Leaf* by James W. Towart;
Copyright by St. Johns Archaelogical Expedition, Inc.
Jacksonville, Florida

Library of Congress Catalogue Number 91-76355

International Standard Book Numbers
Paperbound: 978-1-55613-846-1
Clothbound: 978-0-7884-3410-5

To the memory of my great-grandfather,

Corporal Jeremiah Witt, 10th Arkansas Infantry,

and his brother (and regimental commander)

Colonel Allen Rufus Witt,

one of the Confederate officers on the *Maple Leaf*.

Contents

Introduction

Researching the escape from the Maple Leaf began as a matter of urgent curiosity; the notion of writing about it, however, came more slowly, and completing the writing slower yet. In 1985 I learned of the incident—though not much more than that the escape had occurred. Under the mistaken impression that something has been written on everything that happened during the Civil War, I sought more information, but for many months found only brief sketches of a sentence or two, or at most a few paragraphs. Among these accounts, long and short, however, there were a number of contradictions. I began collecting these bits of information, filling in detail and resolving discrepancies, where possible, as my files grew larger. Somewhere during this process, it occurred to me that I should record my version of the incident, once I felt confident that I had completed sufficient research. I found this a long process, involving many libraries and historical collections, and including graduate study. What follows is the result.

Like many stories set during the Civil War, this is drawn from sources that vary widely in reliability. Probably the most dependable information is that recorded at the time of the event, much of it published in the *Official Record*.[1] Certain other correspondence, private as well as official, together with government documents such as military service and pension records, are generally trustworthy.[2] Next in order of accuracy, with notable exceptions, are contemporary newspaper accounts. Last, in many cases, are the reminiscences of the participants themselves, particularly those which were recorded many years after the war. These personal accounts are invaluable because they provide details found nowhere else, but often their authors' memories had dimmed over the years (particularly regarding dates, distances, names and numbers), sometimes leading them to approximations and even guesses, as a more comfortable choice than simply admitting that the name of a prominent individual or place was lost to memory. Accuracy also suffers from supposition as to what "must have happened," the natural tendency to embellish a story, and finally, bias, which is often difficult to avoid when quoting veterans of the Civil War, North or South.

William Hesseltine noted in 1962 that of all the contentious issues related to the Civil War, none is more controversial, or quicker to raise emotion and bitterness, than the operation of prisons and treatment of prisoners. This story touches on several Union prisons, and quotes the reminiscences of Confederate soldiers confined there. As Professor Hesseltine notes elsewhere, Civil War prisons were typically terrible places owing to their nature, having been unplanned, hurriedly constructed, and inadequately supplied, with resulting infliction of unintended suffering.[3]

Many thousands of Civil War soldiers obtained relief from deplorable prison conditions through the system of exchanges and paroles, which plays a significant role in this story. Although the system is explained in detail at Appendix B, a brief summary is offered here with the hope that it will assist in avoiding confusion.

In July of 1862, Major Generals John A. Dix and Daniel Harvey Hill, representing the Union and the Confederacy respectively, negotiated an agreement (termed a "cartel")[4] calling for prompt exchange of prisoners of war. It provided also, that if one side held prisoners eligible for exchange, but the opposing army had no captives to offer in return, the prisoners might nevertheless be released on "parole," their sworn oath that they would refrain from all actions hostile to their former captors until they were declared to be "exchanged." When the side that initially lacked prisoners to exchange eventually accumulated a sufficient number, it would release them; at the same time, an announcement would be made that an equal number of its own paroled soldiers were considered exchanged and free to take up arms.

Confusion in this story is introduced by practices not sanctioned by the cartel whereby promises (unfortunately—and improperly, in my view—termed paroles) were given and received freely and for practically any purpose. Thus, in this story, some prisoners solemnly promise that they will not try to escape in return for lenient treatment and freedom from close restraint; others, in consideration for being released unharmed, promise to travel to a certain destination. In both cases promises were given (and broken), and although in each case the oath was termed a parole by the parties, they did not constitute paroles in the sense of the agreement.

My purpose is to bring the many accounts of the escape together in one coherent story. While I believe that I have covered the major aspects, I do not claim to have covered them all, nor have I followed every lead. Specifically, I have not fully mined the rich store of oral history available in northeastern North Carolina, or explored the personalities and careers of each of the remarkable group of Confederates held on the ship. Both promise to yield additional curious and fascinating detail. Eight years after starting this project, I am convinced that the abundance of sources is such, that the day will never come when one can say that, "something has been written on everything that happened during the Civil War."

While it is possible to hope that all errors in the manuscript have been found and corrected, experience suggests that this is unlikely, though not for lack of effort.

Notes

1. U.S. War Department, *The War of the Rebellion: A Compilation of the Official Records of the Union and Confederate Armies*, 70 vols. in 128 parts (Washington, D.C.: Government Printing Office (GPO), 1880-1901), hereafter cited as *OR*. This monumental compilation of documents is accompanied by *Official Records of the Union and Confederate Navies in the War of the Rebellion*, 31 vols. (Washington, D.C.: GPO, 1894-1922), hereafter cited as *ORN*, and *Atlas to Accompany the Official Records of the Union and Confederate Armies*(Washington, D.C.: GPO, 1891-1895), hereafter cited as *Atlas to OR*.

2. For a description of the Civil War holdings of the National Archives, see Kenneth W. Munden and Henry Putney Beers, *Guide to Federal Archives Relating to the Civil War*, (Washington, D.C.: GPO, 1962), and as to Southern records, Henry Putney Beers, *Guide to the Archives of the Government of the Confederate States of America*, National Archives Publication No. 68-15, (Washington, D.C.: GPO, 1968).

3. William B. Hesseltine, "Military Prisons of St. Louis, 1861-1965," *The Missouri Historical Review* 23 (April 1929): 380.

4. The Federal government was anxious to avoid any action implying its recognition of the Confederate States. Because of this, the agreement was cast as a cartel (arguably an agreement entered into by opposing armies, as distinct from a treaty, which is one between sovereign nations). In truth though, the agreement remained one between opposing governments or their representatives.

Acknowledgments

As slender as this volume is, it was made possible only by the good will of many people.

I owe much to the late Richard Weinert, for many years an historian employed by the U.S. Army at Fort Monroe, Virginia. Shortly after we met in 1984, he introduced me to sources such as *The Official Record*, and challenged me to venture into the fascinating field of Civil War research.

Without the assistance of Marie Melchiori in searching for specially elusive documents, much of the story could not have been brought to light.

Others who have assisted greatly include David Guinn, of Brighton, Tennessee; Jay Rives Manning, of Roanoke Rapids, North Carolina; Edna Morrisette Shannonhouse, of Elizabeth City, North Carolina; Roger Long of Sandusky, Illinois; Edwin Holloway of Staunton, Virginia; Louis Meekins of Currituck, North Carolina; James Towart of Jacksonville, Florida; James Melchor of Norfolk, Virginia; J. L. Bryan of Grapevine, Texas; and Thomas Parramore of Raleigh, North Carolina. I am also indebted to the staff of Lloyd House, the local history branch of the Alexandria Library, and to the Fort Ward Museum. Help was also provided by Diane Dunford of Lexington, Missouri, and Anne Saba of the U.S. Customs Service. As is true of most who research primary sources relating to the Civil War, I am indebted to the staffs of the Library of Congress, the National Archives and Records Administration, and the U.S. Army Military History Institute.

I am most grateful to Gregory J. W. Urwin, of the University of Central Arkansas, for his endless patience and many valuable suggestions, as well as criticism, advice and encouragement.

The encouragement provided by the faculty of the Department of History at George Mason University contributed to my determination to finish this project. In particular, I am indebted to Joseph L. Harsh, and his contagious enthusiasm for study of the American Civil War.

Others who contributed valued suggestions were Alfred F. Arquilla, and William Hagan of the Washington D.C. area; Marshal G. Kaplan of Brooklyn, New York; and George J. Jacunski, of

Honolulu, Hawaii. Many valuable suggestions were also made by Robert Scott, of Croton-on-Hudson, New York, and Gloria M. Primera of San Antonio, Texas.

General Jay A. Matthews of Austin, Texas granted permission to quote from the Haas translation of the Giesecke diaries published in *Texas Military History*.

The drawing of Fort Norfolk and the maps were prepared by J. Russell Witt of Alexandria, Virginia.

Illustrations

Page 3. Gratiot Street Military Prison, formerly McDowell Medical College, St. Louis, temporary residence of twenty-five to thirty of the Confederate officers in this story who promised that, while on their way to Virginia for exchange, they would not attempt to escape. Courtesy of the Missouri Historical Society, PB18.

Page 6. Shown here while still incomplete, in the spring of 1863, the U.S. Customhouse in New Orleans held fifty of the prisoners who would later be put aboard the *Maple Leaf*. Courtesy of the Historic New Orleans Collection, Museum/Research Center, Acc. No. 87-108-L.

Page 7. Interior sketch showing prisoners in the New Orleans Customhouse. Courtesy of the Historic New Orleans Collection, Museum/Research Center, Acc. No. 1958-43-1287.

Page 10. U.S. transport *Cahawba*, which took the fifty Rebel officers from New Orleans to Fort Monroe. Courtesy of the Military Order of Loyal Legions of the U.S. Army, Massachusetts Commandery, and the U.S. Army Military History Institute (MOLLUS Mass., USAMHI).

Page 11. Deck scene on U.S. transport *Cahawba*, where the Confederate officers enjoyed the hospitality of Colonel Wilson's 6th New York Infantry. Courtesy of the National Archives.

Page 15. Sketch of Fort Monroe Virginia, headquarters of General John A. Dix, and scene of great activity throughout the war. Courtesy of the Mariners Museum, Newport News, Virginia.

Page 16. Col. "Billy" Wilson, 6th New York Infantry, and some of his soldiers. They look a little rough in this photograph, but the Confederate officers on the *Cahawba* thought highly of them. Courtesy of MOLLUS Mass., USAMHI.

Page 18. U.S. transport *Utica* before the war. After being taken off the *Cahawba*, the prisoners from New Orleans passed the night of June 8, 1863, on this ship before being put aboard the *Maple Leaf* the next morning. Courtesy of the Mariners Museum, Newport News, Virginia.

Page 20. Col. Roberts, 3d Pennsylvania (Heavy) Artillery, and some of his staff in 1864, by which time one his officers, Lieutenant William E. Dorsey, had been dismissed for dereliction. Courtesy of MOLLUS Mass., USAMHI.

Page 22. The only known photograph of the *Maple Leaf*, taken in 1856 by Edward Whitney. Courtesy of Gerald T. Girvin of Rochester, N.Y.

Page 30. Captioned only "Captain of the Maple Leaf," this is believed to be Henry W. Dale, who commanded the ship during its Civil War service. Courtesy of MOLLUS Mass., USAMHI.

Page 32. Line drawing of the *Maple Leaf* by James W. Towart. Courtesy of St. Johns Archaeological Expedition, Inc., Jacksonville, Florida.

Page 34. Lieutenant Dorsey's "parole." By terms of documents such as this, the Rebels hoped they would bind the officers on the *Maple Leaf* to proceed to Fort Delaware without reporting the escape. Courtesy of the National Archives.

Page 45. Brigadier General Michael Corcoran, who sent cavalry under Major James Wheelan to intercept the prisoners from the *Maple Leaf*. A tragic figure who had recently killed a fellow officer, Corcoran was himself killed in a riding accident a short time later. Courtesy of the Library of Congress.

Page 55. Confederate Secretary of War James A. Seddon, who urged General D. H. Hill to assist the fugitives from the *Maple Leaf*. Many visitors commented on Seddon's unhealthy appearance, but he outlived most of them. Courtesy of the National Archives.

Page 56. Confederate General Daniel Harvey Hill, the Rebel negotiator of the cartel on paroles and exchanges, whose troops sought to assist those from the *Maple Leaf.* Courtesy of the Library of Congress.

Page 58. Union commander at Fort Monroe, General John A. Dix, who negotiated the agreement on paroles and exchanges, and who was responsible for the prisoners on the *Maple Leaf.* Courtesy of the Library of Congress.

Page 64. In a moment of exuberance, when being paid in Richmond, Col. Allen Rufus Witt scrawled the fact of his escape across the face of his pay voucher. Courtesy of the National Archives.

Page 66. Col. Allen Rufus Witt, from composite photograph, "Senate Memorial, 1866-7," by T. W. Banks, Little Rock. Courtesy of the Arkansas History Commission.

Page 75. Major Oliver Semmes, shown here after the war, was the elected leader of the escaped prisoners from the *Maple Leaf.* Courtesy of the Museum of Mobile.

Page 78. The colorful Californian, Judge "Ned" McGowan. Accustomed to evading pursuers, San Francisco's Vigilance Committee had spent months searching for him, without success. A natural storyteller, he often entertained his companions with tales of his adventures. Courtesy of the Library of Congress.

Page 83. Fort Norfolk, Virginia. From here, forty-seven Confederate prisoners were marched aboard the *Maple Leaf.* Some of those from St. Louis felt the harsh treatment received here justified breaking their promise not to attempt an escape. Courtesy of James Melchor, Norfolk District, U.S. Army Corps of Engineers.

Page 84. Plan of Fort Norfolk, based on drawings in the Cartographic Division, NARA, RG 77, Civil Works Map File, and RG 74, Bureau of Ordnance, Navy Department, November 22, 1852.

Page 86. Spotswood Hotel, Richmond, where many of the escaped Confederates rested and "had a good time." Once the most elegant hotel in Richmond, this photograph was taken at the end of the war. Courtesy of the Library of Congress.

Page 87. Johnson's Island as sketched by Union guard Edward Gould. The eventual destination of at least fifteen of those on the *Maple Leaf*. Several died here within a few weeks. Courtesy of Don Young, Sandusky, Ohio.

Page 88. Contemporary sketch of prisoners arriving at Fort Delaware, the intended destination of the ninety-seven Confederates on the *Maple Leaf*. Courtesy of MOLLUS Mass., USAMHI.

Page 89. Fort Delaware today, considerably modified since the Civil War, is a state park. The wood barracks which housed most of the prisoners, as many as 12,000 at a time, was located some 100 yards to the left (north-west) of the structure shown here, and disappeared long ago. Courtesy of Fort Delaware State Park.

Maps

Facing title page. Eastern United States. Places having a role in the story of the *Maple Leaf*.

Page 47. Vicinity of southeastern Virginia and northeastern North Carolina. Area traversed by Confederates escaping from the *Maple Leaf*.

Chapter 1

Difficult to Describe Our Feelings

In the third year of the Civil War, off the Virginia coast near Cape Henry, ninety-seven Rebel officers, unwilling passengers on the U.S. transport *Maple Leaf*, were on their way north to join the many other Southerners held in the Federal prisoner of war camp at Fort Delaware. This is their story.

By June of 1863, the war had raged for over two years, and fortune was shifting rapidly in favor of the North. Union armies surrounded and were laying siege to Southern garrisons on the Mississippi River at Vicksburg and Port Hudson. The previous September at Antietam, the Confederacy suffered heavy losses in the single bloodiest day of the war. Although three months later, at Fredericksburg, the Union Army had sustained nearly as many casualties, it had available a much larger pool of replacement manpower. For the South, return of its captured soldiers was particularly important.

Earlier during the war, prisoners were regularly exchanged or released on parole at City Point, Virginia, and Vicksburg, Mississippi, as agreed upon by the cartel. This story deals with two groups of Rebel officers held by the North, for convenience designated here as the Fort Norfolk Group and the New Orleans Group.

The Fort Norfolk Group

Forty-seven officers were among the Union Army's prisoners at Fort Norfolk, Virginia. Located on the Elizabeth River, the fort had been constructed in the early nineteenth century for the defense of Portsmouth, as well as Norfolk, but had fallen into disuse. Taken over by the Navy as an ammunition depot in the 1850s, the Confederates captured it soon after the war began. With the fall of Norfolk in May of 1862, however, the Union Army again occupied the fort, and used portions of it as a hospital and prison.[1] From the "Fort Norfolk Jail," it was convenient to put the prisoners on "flag of truce" boats for transportation down the Elizabeth River to the James, then up the James to the designated exchange site at City Point, only some sixty-five miles away.

There, the Union Army would deliver the Rebel prisoners to Confederates officials in return for Federal soldiers.

The Confederate officers held at Fort Norfolk, awaiting transportation to City Point and release on exchange, fell into three categories. The largest was composed of twenty-five to thirty men who had been sent there from St. Louis. A second consisted of prisoners who had arrived from Fort Delaware, the large seacoast fort and prison located on Peapatch Island in the Delaware River, near Wilmington. The third category was made up of those who arrived individually or in small bands, having been captured at various places in the eastern theater of operations.

The prisoners from St. Louis had been held in that city's Gratiot Street Military Prison. Formerly the McDowell Medical College, early in the war Union officials confiscated the building from its Southern-sympathizing owner, and used it to confine Confederate prisoners of war and Northern offenders as well, both military and civilian.[2] Before sending the Rebel prisoners east for exchange, their captors asked them to take an oath, which they termed a "parole," promising that they would not attempt to escape. In return, the Union officials offered the prisoners assurances that they would be well treated, and allowed a liberal degree of freedom from close restraint. The Rebels readily agreed to these conditions.

On June 5, the prisoners left the Gratiot Street Prison and were ferried across to the east bank of the Mississippi River. From there, they travelled by rail through Indianapolis, Cincinnati, and Harrisburg, to Baltimore. They then boarded a British steamer for Norfolk, which they considered an intermediate stop on their way to City Point and release on parole or exchange. Soon after their arrival at Fort Norfolk on June 7, however, the prisoners were told that paroles and exchanges had been suspended, and that they would remain at Fort Norfolk until they could be sent north to Fort Delaware, the Northern prison mentioned earlier.[3] "It would be difficult to describe our feeling," one of the prisoners wrote, telling of the deep despair they felt upon learning that, contrary to their hopes of many days, now grown to expectations, freedom was not soon at hand.[4]

Conditions at the Fort Norfolk Jail were as bad as at other Civil War prisons, mostly due to severe overcrowding and lack of

sanitation. Those who had traveled from St. Louis found things quite different from what they had been accustomed to on their trip across the country and what they had come to expect was their due. A Richmond newspaper reported:

> The prisoners were all put in small rooms, eighteen officers being shut up in a room fifteen feet square, which had but one little grated window so high as to be out of reach. A guard was placed at the door, which was only open long enough to hand them their meanest of fare.[5]

As mentioned earlier, in addition to those who arrived from the Gratiot Street Prison, the Fort Norfolk jail held several men who had recently arrived from Fort Delaware, the construction of which had only been completed in 1860. Though designed for seacoast protection, during the Civil War it was used primarily as a prison, with as many as 12,000 Rebel soldiers quartered in wooden barracks adjacent to the fort proper.[6]

The men from Fort Delaware, like Captain Wynne Cannon, who had been captured at Murfreesboro, Tennessee, nearly six months earlier, knew that they had been sent south to be exchanged, and were probably the most disappointed at learning they would have to return to the same prison they had so recently left. Fort Delaware was the newly announced destination of the other Confederate officers at Fort Norfolk as well.[7]

Among them were:

o First Lieutenant Thomas E. Moss, 2d Kentucky Infantry. Age twenty-four, this veteran of Fort Donelson, also fell into Union hands during at Murfreesboro on January 2, 1863.[8]

o Lieutenant Colonel John Uriah Green, 12th Tennessee Cavalry. Thirty-two years old at the time of his capture in Shelby County, Tennessee, on April 8, 1863, Green had enlisted as a private, and risen from the ranks.[9]

o Captain Richard T. Seckel, a native of Pennsylvania, pioneer settler of California, and veteran of William Walker's 1855 filibustering expedition to Nicaragua. Seckel, thirty-three, was Provost Marshal of the Southeastern Department of Missouri until he was captured at Bloomfield, on March 1, 1863, in a pre-dawn raid by the 2d Missouri State Militia Cavalry led by Lieutenant Frederick Poole.[10]

4

o Captain Ai Edgar Asbury, 6th Missouri Cavalry, former aide de camp to Brigadier General James H. McBride, captured on April 20, 1863, while in northern Missouri on recruiting service. Asbury, twenty-four, was a school commissioner in Houston, Texas County, Missouri, and in his first year of law practice when the war began. He had seen action at the battle of Wilson's Creek, and was nearby when Union Major General Nathaniel Lyon was killed.[11]

o Captain Edward S. Parker, Commissary of the 50th North Carolina, captured on April 16, 1863. Age twenty-three, and living in Goldsboro, North Carolina, Parker's first year of practicing law had also been interrupted by the war.[12]

These are but a few of the prisoners confined at Fort Norfolk, whose hopes of release had been ruined by news of the suspension of exchanges and paroles.

Some of the prisoners at Fort Norfolk, though disappointed at the suspension of exchanges, nevertheless were looking forward with hope to an improvement in their living conditions once they reached Fort Delaware. They were unaware, however, that several hundred miles away, in New Orleans, another group of prisoners, very much like themselves, had been assembled and was on its way north, a matter that would have an important bearing on their future.

The New Orleans Group

Confederate prisoners in New Orleans were held in the U.S. Customhouse. Trained in engineering at West Point, Pierre G. T. Beauregard began supervising the building's construction in 1849, and it was still far from complete when the war began. When the city was occupied by Union troops in May of 1862, a portion of the building was converted into a prison. Another part served as headquarters of Major General Benjamin F. Butler, the city's Federal commander who had, during the 1860 Democratic Convention, steadfastly voted through fifty-seven ballots for his candidate, Jefferson Davis. It was at the customhouse, in December 1862, that Butler, by then despised by many Southerners and within a few days of being declared an outlaw by Jefferson Davis, relinquished his position as commander of the Department of the Gulf.[13]

U. S. CUSTOM HOUSE,
(FRONTING ON CANAL STREET.)
NEW ORLEANS.

Most of the Rebels held at the Customhouse, as many as 2,000 at a time, occupied large rooms on the unfinished upper story of the building, though when great numbers of prisoners were passing through, smaller rooms were used as well. One of these men later complained that he and his companions were put in a "little hold with but one window covered with iron bars. The place was so small that we could scarcely find room to lie down and the odor was terrible, so bad that we could not at first stand it."[14] Another wrote, however, that "our lodgings . . . were not the most comfortable in the world, but they were warm and dry, and that was much."[15]

By June 1, the prisoners at the Customhouse included a large number of Confederate officers. On June 2, Federal authorities selected fifty of them for shipment to Fort Monroe—and, the prisoners hoped—to City Point for exchange. According to one of them, Captain A. Porter Morse, they were moved hurriedly and in secret to avoid public demonstrations of support for the Confederacy, to a tug boat waiting at the foot of Canal Street. The tug ferried them to the *Cahawba*, a sea-going transport anchored nearby. As soon as the prisoners were on board, the *Cahawba* got underway. Morse noted in his diary, "The *Cahawba* swings clear of the wharf and sweeps down the Mississippi just as the dying sunlight gilds the spires of church and chapel."[16]

A 250-foot side-wheeler, the *Cahawba* had already been in service for seven years, plying between New Orleans, Texas, and San Juan. When the war began she was chartered by the Union Army for $500-800 a day.[17] The fifty Rebel officers she now carried had been captured during various engagements in the Federal Army's Department of the Gulf. Their escort during the voyage north was the 6th New York Volunteer Infantry. Under the command of Colonel William Wilson, the regiment, also known as "Wilson's Zouaves," had been a part of the Union forces operating against Port Hudson when the soldiers' enlistments expired, and they were on their way home to New York for discharge, or "mustering out." They were nearly as happy to be leaving Louisiana, as the Rebels were to be free of the Customhouse.[18]

On board the *Cahawba*, Captain Morse noted in his diary, "as I pace the deck of this staunch ship, catch the fresh breezes of the

8

Gulf, and look out upon the bright sunlight again, my lungs fill, my head clears, and the effects of a long fever which has prostrated me for weeks begin to pass away. I share these sensations with most of my fellow-prisoners, and the fire returns to many an eye that had grown dull and dim with confinement."

Unlike the group of prisoners mentioned earlier (those sent to Fort Norfolk from St. Louis), the fifty Confederate officers in Wilson's charge on the *Cahawba* had not promised to cooperate with their captors. On the other hand, for prisoners, they could hardly have been more comfortable. Federal authorities had decided to give them the same privileges as their own officers, and treated them "better than they had any right or reason to expect."[19] For their part, the Yankees enjoyed their Rebel guests:

These gentlemen the Sixth found a very pleasant lot of fellows, and as it is much pleasanter to drink and exchange yarns with a man than to shoot at him, the officers and men got on the best of terms with their friends the enemy, and this companionship did much to lessen the monotony of the voyage to Fortress Monroe.[20]

The Confederates, too, enjoyed the voyage. In his diary entry for June 4, Morse note, "clear and pleasant with light wind. Entertained by the antics of the pet of the regiment (a fine goat brought from New York, and with the regiment during their travels and marches); 'Billy' seems to take equally to sugar or tobacco, whiskey or salt water. . . . Making ten knots all day."

Of the officers shipped from New Orleans, several had been captured in southern Louisiana in connection with the battle of Irish Bend. There, in early April 1863, Major General Nathaniel P. Banks attempted to encircle a Confederate Army under Major General Richard Taylor. Banks, forty-seven, a former governor of Massachusetts, and member of the U.S. House of Representatives, had been given the goal of capturing Port Hudson, Louisiana, a mission he would accomplish three months later. First, however, he attempted to open the Red River to the Federal Army. His opponent, Taylor, was ten years younger, a brother-in-law of Jefferson Davis, and son of President Zachary Taylor, for whom General Taylor had served as military secretary during the Mexican War.

9

Taylor's force occupied a narrow strip of land between the Atchafalaya River (which broadens into Grand Lake) and the Bayou Teche. His flanks were guarded on his left by the ram *Queen of the West* in the Atchafalaya, and on his right by the gunboat *Diana* in the Teche, both vessels having recently been captured from Union forces. Banks adopted a plan calling for a frontal assault against Taylor's forces, while at the same time sending an encircling army by way of Grand Lake to land in Taylor's rear, blocking his retreat up the Teche. The encircling force was delayed, however, and Taylor became alert to the danger. He feigned a defense at the point of Banks' frontal assault, and threw his main effort against the encircling force. This enabled him to withdraw with his main body of men, outnumbered approximately three to one, up the Teche toward Alexandria. Among the Confederates captured during these operations were:

o Captain Oliver Semmes, of the 1st Confederate Regular Light Artillery Battery, son of Confederate Navy Captain Raphael Semmes of the commerce raider *Alabama*.[21] Because Oliver Semmes was an experienced artilleryman, Taylor placed him in charge of the gunboat *Diana* just two days before, when its commander became ill. Later during the fighting, Semmes scuttled the *Diana* to prevent the vessel falling back into Federal hands. In describing his command's escape from General Banks, Taylor concluded his report saying, "Captain Semmes, in command of the *Diana*, and his crew conducted themselves with the greatest bravery and intrepidity, and deserve the highest encomiums."[22]

o Captain Emelius W. Fuller, commander of the *Queen of the West*. Fuller was wounded and captured with the destruction of his ship, which guarded Taylor's left flank.[23] Union Admiral David G. Farragut paid a compliment to Fuller when he cabled a subordinate, "I am glad that our people have had a little success on the Teche, etc., and that the Clifton banged [*sic*] the Queen of the West and with her the great fighter, Captain Fuller." Because of his exploits Fuller had been referred to by one newspaper as "the Paul Jones of the South," and Confederate Secretary of State Judah P. Benjamin had tried, without success, to have him promoted.[24] It was said that, before the war, Fuller was a member of the Louisiana legislature and at one time a candidate for Governor.[25]

12

o Captain Julius Giesecke, twenty-four years old, from New Braunfels, Texas, commander of Company G, 4th Texas Cavalry. Like many of his neighbors back home, Giesecke was born in Germany, and came to the U.S. as a youth. His company—all of whom spoke German—elected him their commander in February 1862, after Captain Marinus van der Heuvel lost his life in a cavalry charge at Valverde. By the time of his capture at Irish Bend on April 14, Giesecke had seen considerable action, leading his men in battle at La Glorieta Pass, and in the recapture of Galveston.[26]

o Captain Leclerc Fusilier, a wealthy plantation owner, who, despite his more than sixty years, was a volunteer aide on General Taylor's staff. Taylor's report complimented Fusilier's performance in the battle, saying that he was "always under fire, carrying orders, enduring fatigue, hurrying up caissons when the severity of the fire made the drivers hesitate . . . ." He later wrote, "the first gun seemed to signal for the appearance of Captain Fusilier who, on his white pony, could be seen where the fighting was the thickest leading on or encouraging his neighbors."[27]

o Edward "Ned" McGowan, Arizona Brigade, attached to the gunboat *Diana*. Politician, poet, and lawyer, Ned was well known throughout the country for having escaped San Francisco's Committee of Vigilance which had accused him of complicity in the murder of a newspaper publisher, James King of William, in June, 1856. After evading the committee, which even Governor William Johnson, assisted by Major General William T. Sherman of the California Militia, was unable to bring under control, McGowan submitted to authorities a year later. He was tried and acquitted with the jury requiring only ten minutes for its deliberation. His subsequent journeys took him to Mexico and then Arizona, where he was designated the territory's representative to the Confederate convention. He then joined Sibley's Arizona Brigade, which was absorbed into the 4th Texas Brigade. (McGowan's brother, John, in the U.S. maritime service, was also well known from the time when he was master of the *Star of the West* when it was fired upon while attempting to deliver supplies to Fort Sumpter in January 1861.)[28]

Describing the events of April 14, General Banks jubilantly wrote to Major General Ulysses S. Grant:

> The gunboats Diana, Hart, and Queen of the West have been destroyed and their armament captured by our forces. We have among our prisoners the most important officers of all arms, Captain Fuller, the commander of their fleet, captured from the Queen of the West, known here as the 'King of the Swamp,' long in the legislature and at the head of the filibuster or fighting element of the state, whose candidate he was for the office of Governor. We have also Captain Semmes, the first officer of their artillery.[29]

Others prisoners on board the *Cahawba* had been captured at such diverse places as:

o Baton Rouge, Louisiana - First Lieutenant David N. Estes, 9th Tennessee Cavalry Battalion, caught by Federals while patrolling near that city. Estes had once before fallen into enemy hands with the fall of Fort Donelson and had been exchanged at Vicksburg.[30]

o Port Hudson, Louisiana - Colonel Allen Rufus Witt, of the 10th Arkansas Infantry. Witt was thirty-three at the time of his capture, on May 27, 1863, during the early phase of the first major Federal assault on Port Hudson. Two of his officers and nearly fifty enlisted members of the regiment were taken with him.[31]

Six days after departing New Orleans, the *Cahawba* reached Hampton Roads, where, on June 8, it dropped anchor near the brooding stone citadel of Fort Monroe. An impressive feat of military engineering, the fort was designed to employ 380 guns, with a moat eight feet deep and sixty to one hundred and fifty feet wide, surrounding an area of sixty-three acres.[32] Captain Giesecke wrote in his diary, that the *Cahawba* "went right on to Fortress Monroe where we arrived at 1:30 p.m. and anchors were thrown out. . . . The natural as well as the artificial scenery around us was grand; only regret it very much that one cannot enjoy it in freedom."[33]

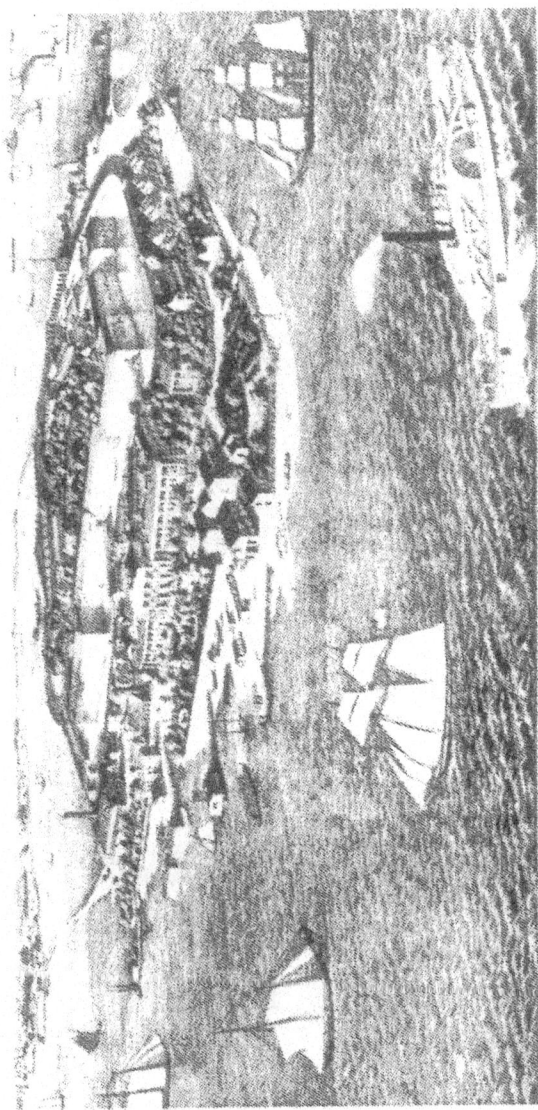

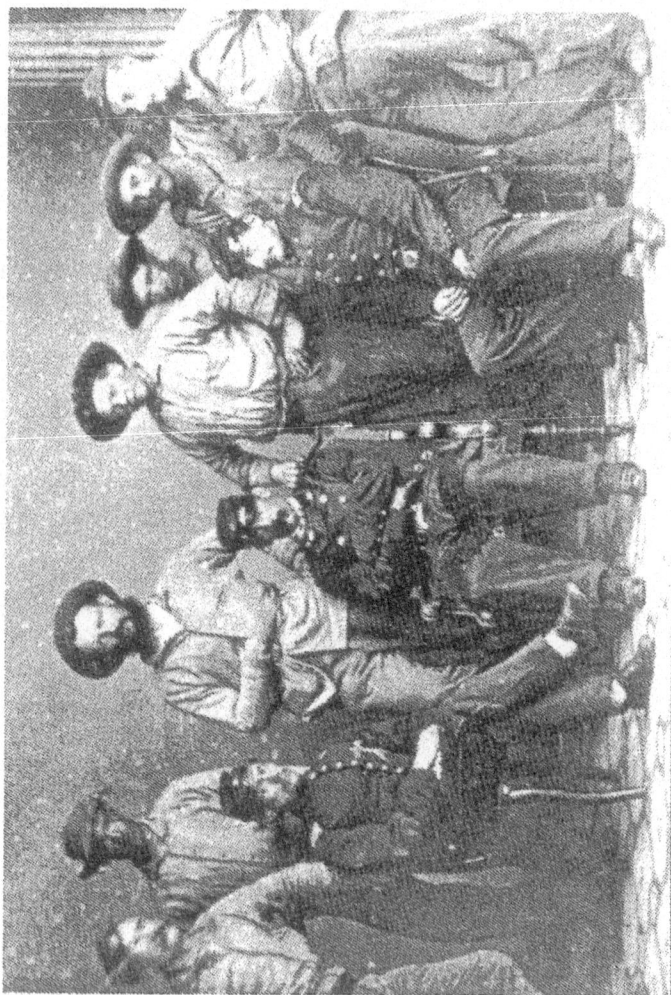

Just before the Confederates left the *Cahawba*, Captain Fuller asked Lieutenant McGowan to chair a committee, with Captain Holmes as secretary, to prepare a resolution of thanks to Colonel Wilson and his men. The committee, composed of Colonel Witt, Lieutenant Morse, and Captains Fuller, Semmes, Fusilier, Youngblood, and Atkinson, produced a draft resolution, unusual under any circumstances, but rare for its characterization of the 6th New York, which the Rebel officers adopted unanimously:

> *Resolved*, That we tender our gratitude and thanks
> to Col. Wm. Wilson, his officers and men of the
> 6th N.Y. Vol., for the kind and courteous treatment
> received at their hands during our passage from
> New Orleans to Fortress Monroe.[34]

Although they may have enjoyed Colonel Wilson's hospitality on board the *Cahawba*, the other Confederate officers felt the same as Giesecke and were looking forward to freedom, although with some anxiety, since they were really not sure what would happen next. Captain Morse noted that, "this was a gloomy day, full of apprehension and uncertainty, mingled with regret at parting with soldiers whose consideration for prisoners was in striking contrast to that hitherto experienced or expected."

Upon its arrival at Fort Monroe, the *Cahawba* was met by news reporters who sent their employers stories of the Wilson's Zouaves and their Confederate "guests." Thereafter, the Yankees moved the prisoners to the *Utica*, described by Captain Giesecke as "an old river boat." The ship, once an elegant river steamer, had already been in service for nearly thirty years, but with the coming of war, her continued employment was required by the Army. One hundred and eighty feet in length, the old side-wheeler provided ample accommodation for the Rebels transferred from the *Cahawba*, whose other passengers were in a hurry to proceed to their homes in New York.[35]

After spending the night of June 8, confined on the *Utica*, the Confederates were surprised to find themselves being moved again, this time to the transport *Maple Leaf*, another large side-wheel steamer. The *Maple Leaf* was preparing to sail, pursuant to orders received from Fort Monroe.[36]

The commanding general at Fort Monroe, Headquarters of the Federal Army's VII Corps, was Major General John A. Dix. A

sixty-five-year-old veteran of the War of 1812, and former U.S. senator and secretary of the treasury, Dix had several years' military experience, primarily as a junior officer. He was considered an able administrator, but by the time of the Civil War, he was thought by many to be too old for field command.

Upon the arrival of the *Cahawba* at Fort Monroe, Dix was handed a letter written by Brigadier General James Bowen, Provost Marshal of New Orleans, the same day the ship sailed from that city. Bowen recommended that the prisoners not be exchanged or paroled because of a decision by the Confederate government that officers captured in the Department of the Gulf would be turned over to local state authorities.[37] Bowen's letter probably made little difference, however, since by that time it was likely that Dix had received orders from Washington suspending exchanges and paroles.

As soon as the prisoners from the *Utica* were on board the *Maple Leaf*, the ship departed for nearby Fort Norfolk. She arrived there about 4:00 P.M., and anchored for the night. The prisoners were still under the impression that they were destined for City Point and exchange, and wishful thinking prompted rumors, untrue, that the *Maple Leaf* was regularly used as a "flag of truce boat."

Early the next morning, June 10, the forty-seven prisoners from Fort Norfolk were marched aboard the *Maple Leaf* to join those from New Orleans. Captain Asbury, who was ill, was one of those brought aboard at Fort Norfolk, thinking at the time that Fort Delaware would be an improvement. He later noted that he and his companions "were surprised and much gratified at the order to prepare for removal to Fort Delaware, and at once were taken out into the fresh, glorious air and placed upon the magnificent United States Steamer 'Maple Leaf,' which was passing on her way from New Orleans [*sic*] to Fort Delaware."[38]

Once the prisoners from Fort Norfolk were aboard, the ship returned to Fort Monroe.[39] It was about this time that the Confederates from New Orleans first learned that they were not going to be released, but were on their way to Fort Delaware. That afternoon, June 10, at 1:00 P.M., the *Maple Leaf* once again sailed from Fort Monroe. It now carried a total of ninety-seven Confederate officers, and by this time, all knew its destination.

Although those from New Orleans were disappointed to learn that they would not be exchanged, the news was not greatly surprising to some of them. Captain Giesecke had noted in his diary entry of April 17, nearly two months before and just three days after his capture, that, "only one thing bothered me a little and that was the proclamation of President Davis (that no officers would be exchanged and he would have officers shot if General Butler was not released [to Confederate authorities])".

Doubtless, others were equally aware of Davis's proclamation, and harbored a secret dread—despite hope to the contrary—that they might be denied exchange or parole in retaliation.

The prisoners consolidated on the *Maple Leaf* were a varied lot (see roster at Appendix A). Ranging in grade from second lieutenant to colonel,[40] they represented over sixty-five regiments, and, some claimed, every state of the Confederacy. It is likely that these officers displayed a confusing but colorful variety of clothing, considering the lack of standardized dress within the Confederate Army. Referring to the prisoners who arrived at Fort Monroe on the *Cahawba*, the *Washington Evening Star* reported that the men "wore new and costly uniforms," that they were "seemingly well educated," and "had plenty of money about them."[41] By now, however, the morale of the prisoners was at its lowest. With their varied backgrounds, they now all knew that the one thing they all had in common was the dismal prospect of life in prison, possibly until the end of the war.

The prisoners' escort for the voyage north was very different from the one that brought the fifty men from New Orleans to Fort Monroe on the *Cahawba*. Rather than a regiment of several hundred men, it consisted only of a twelve-man guard detail commanded by Second Lieutenant William E. Dorsey, of the 3d Pennsylvania (Heavy) Artillery. Just the day before his departure for Fort Delaware, Dorsey, a native of Harrisburg, Pennsylvania, had been enjoying garrison duty with his regiment at Camp Hamilton, only a mile or so from Fort Monroe.[42] That morning he received orders to proceed with the prisoners on the *Maple Leaf* to Fort Norfolk, there to pick up more prisoners, and to deliver them all to Fort Delaware. He was assisted by Thomas B. Burnie, Sergeant of the Guard.[43] As the *Maple Leaf* sailed out of Chesapeake Bay, Dorsey had no idea that the events which were

21

about to occur during this mission—one that he had no knowledge of twenty-four hours earlier—would play a crucial role in his brief Army career.

Notes

1. Emanuel Raymond Lewis, *Seacoast Fortifications of the United States* (Washington, D.C.: Smithsonian Institution Press, 1970) pp. 26, 28. James Melchor, *Fort Norfolk*, unpublished history of Fort Norfolk in files of author.

2. Hesseltine, "Military Prisons of St. Louis," 383.

3. One of the major breakdowns in the system of exchanges and paroles occurred toward the end of May 1863. The first steps toward disrupting the system occurred in response to General Pope's ordering Southern sympathizers off their lands under penalty of being hanged as spies; Jefferson Davis reacted by issuing a decree (never implemented) excepting certain Union officers and their subordinates from the benefits of the cartel. Then, reacting to Lincoln's preliminary emancipation proclamation in September of 1862, and the recruitment of the first black soldiers, Davis announced a policy (also never implemented) that captured Union officers commanding black soldiers would be delivered to local state authorities for trial as common criminals inciting servile insurrection. At the same time, because of what Davis viewed as criminal conduct, he declared Major General Benjamin Butler to be an "outlaw," and exempted him from the benefits of the cartel. Stanton retaliated, at first, by suspending the exchange of officers—also not fully implemented. Bickering continued, and on May 25, 1863, Stanton directed the suspension of all paroles and exchanges—yet another policy not fully implemented, but one which prevented the release of the Rebel officers in this story. Halleck to Dix, et. al., May 25, 1863, *OR*, Series 2, vol. 5, p. 696.

4. John Uriah Green, *My Life in Prison and Escape - A Story of the Civil War*, ed. J. G. Whitten, (Navasota, Tex.: Navasota Examiner Review, 1952), p. 23. This compilation of Colonel Green's accounts of his experiences during the Civil War was published initially as a series of articles in the *Tipton County Record* in 1886. They formed the basis for numerous other short accounts, such as "Prison Life and Escape of Col. Green," *Confederate Veteran* 7 (January 1898): 57; and "Thrilling Incident - Capture of the Federal Steamer Maple Leaf," *Southern Historical Society Papers*, hereafter cited as *SHSP*, 24 (January - December 1896): 165-71, quoting from the *Richmond Dispatch* of April 26, 1896. Another is W. B. Browne, "Stranger than Fiction: Capture of the United States Steamer Maple Leaf, Near Cape Henry, Half a Century Ago," *SHSP*, 39 (April 1914): 181-85. This account draws heavily on the various versions of Colonel Green's adventures.

5. *The Daily Richmond Inquirer*, June 23, 1863. At about this time, on June 15, Lieutenant Colonel J. K. Barnes, a U.S. Army medical inspector, reported, concerning the Fort Norfolk jail, "Clothing of prisoners dirty and worn. * * * The overcrowding of the prison cannot be controlled by the immediate commander. If a number of prisoners arrive it must hold them, whether 100 or 500, and the risk of thus developing a contagious epidemic proportionably [sic] increases with the advance of the season." *OR*, Series 2, vol. 6, p. 20.

6. Federal Writers' Project of the Works Progress Administration, *Delaware, a Guide to the First State* (New York: Viking Press, 1938), pp. 471-73. W. Emerson Wilson, *Fort Delaware*, (Wilmington, Del.: Old Wilmington Printing Co., 1955; repr. William P. Frank, ed., Fort Delaware Historical Society, 1983).

7. Clement A. Evans, ed., *Confederate Military History* (Atlanta: Confederate Publishing Co., 1899; repr. Wilmington, N.C.: Broadfoot Publishing Co., 1987), hereafter cited as *CMH*, vol. 10, *Arkansas*, by John Harrell, p. 393-94. Conditions at Fort Delaware were probably not better than Fort Norfolk. On June 15, 1863, the Fort Delaware commander wrote the Surgeon General, "Four thousand rebel prisoners here. Too many sick for two acting assistant surgeons." Schoepf to Hammond, June 15, 1863, *OR*, Series 2, vol. 6, p. 20. The next month, Quartermaster General Montgomery Meigs telegraphed his assistant in Philadelphia, "Send a steam water-boat to Fort Delaware for service while so many prisoners are continued there. It is reported that the water is not good, and that there is much sickness attributed to the use of water, producing diarrhea." Meigs to Crosman, July 11, 1863, *OR*, Series 2, vol. 6, p. 104.

8. *CMH*, vol. 11, *Kentucky*, by J. Stoddard Johnston, pp. 482-83.

9. J. G. Whitten, introduction to Green, *Life in Prison and Escape*. Joseph H. Crute, Jr., *Units of the Confederate States Army* (Midlothian, Va.: Derwent Books, 1987), pp. 286-87.

10. Mamie Yeary, comp., *Reminiscences of the Boys in Gray, 1861-1865* (Dallas: Smith and Lamar, 1912) p. 675. *Richmond Daily Examiner*, June 23, 1863. *Confederate Veteran* 28 (April 1920): 148. Poole to McNiel, March 3, 1863, *OR*, Series 1, vol. 22, pt. 1, p. 235.

11. *Confederate Veteran*, 20 (May 1912): 242, "My Experiences in the War of 1861-1862," note pertaining to Ai Edgar Asbury. Thomas R. Gibson, "Gen. James H. McBride," *Confederate Veteran* 23 (August 1915): 375. Ai Edgar Asbury, *My Experiences in the War 1861 to 1865* (Kansas City, Mo.: Berkowitz & Co., 1894), p. 3.

12. *Confederate Veteran* 23 (January 1915): 41, note pertaining to Edward S. Parker. *CMH*, vol. 5, *North Carolina*, by D. H. Hill, Jr., pp. 681-83.

13. Samuel Wilson, Jr., *A History of the U.S. Customhouse in New Orleans* (New Orleans: U.S. Custom Service, Region V, 1982), pp. 53-58. Federal Writers' Project of the works Progress Administration, *New Orleans City Guide* (Boston: Houghton Mifflin Company, 1938), pp. 268-69.

14. Oscar Haas, trans. and ed. "Diary of Julius Giesecke, 1863-1865," *Texas Military History* 4 (Spring 1964): 30. Giesecke's diary was originally published in *Jahrbuch der New-Braunfelser Zeitung, für 1934 - 1935*.

15. John Smith Kendall, ed. "Recollections of a Confederate Officer," [John Irwin Kendall], *The Louisiana Historical Quarterly* 29 (October 1946): 1041-1141.

16. A. Porter Morse, "The Capture of the 'Maple Leaf'," William Browne, ed., *The Southern Magazine*, September 1871, pp. 302-09. "The Cahawba was announced to sail north last evening with the Wilson Zouaves whose term of enlistment expired in April, and with several Confederate prisoners who are to be left at Fortress Monroe for exchange." *The New Orleans Daily Picayune*, June 3, 1863.

17. Eric Heyl, *Early American Steamers* (Buffalo: Eric Heyl, 1953), vol. 1, pp. 65-66.

18. Wilson's 6th New York Zouaves were widely regarded as undisciplined brawlers, as tough as the Bowery could produce. On the evening of March 26, 1863, at Baton Rouge, they marched on board the steam transport *Morning Light*, which was to take them to Donaldsonville. Heavy drinking led to rowdiness, and eventually an all-night rampage—some called it a mutiny—causing great damage and loss of property, to the ship as well as its crew. The soldiers probably thought they had a grand time, but their brigade commander, Brigadier General William Dwight, was furious. He claimed that Wilson was sleeping in his cabin throughout the melee, and charged the colonel with dereliction of duty for his failure to keep order. There was probably little that Wilson could have done once the party began, however, and some of his officers were assaulted by the drunken soldiers; indeed, it was alleged that several of Wilson's officers foresaw what was about to happen, and took another steamer to Donaldsonville. NARA, CSR, William Wilson, 6th New York Infantry.

19. "They [the Confederate officers held on the *Cahawba*] are mostly of gentlemanly appearance and dress, and by Gen. Emory's orders [were] placed on a par with U.S. officers on board the transport . . . ." *New York Daily Tribune*, June 11, 1863. Brigadier General William H. Emory was the Federal commander in charge of the defense of New Orleans.

20. Gouverneur Morris, *The History of a Volunteer Regiment - Being a Succinct Account of the Organization, Services and Adventures of the Sixth Regiment New*

York Volunteer Infantry Known as Wilson's Zouaves (New York: Veteran Volunteer Pub. Co., 1891), p. 114.

21. A cadet in his third year at the U.S. Military Academy when the war began, Captain Semmes was appointed to command one of the few units of the Confederate Regular Army. See Richard P. Weinert, Jr., *The Confederate Regular Army* (Shippensburg, Pa.: White Mane Publishing Company, 1991), which also provides an excellent account of the battle at Irish Bend at pp. 61-76. See also, *CMH*, vol. 8, *Alabama*, by Joseph Wheeler, pp. 794-95. He was seldom mentioned, either in the press or in private correspondence, without reference to his famous father, sometimes in complimentary terms, though Northern papers often referred to him as "a son of the rebel pirate." *New York Times*, June 14, 1863.

22. Taylor to Boggs, April 23, 1863, *ORN*, Series 1, vol. 20, pp. 822-25.

23. For an account of the battle and destruction of the *Queen of the West* in Grand Lake on April 14, 1863, see Cooke to Morris, April 15, 1863, *ORN*, Series 1, vol. 20, pp. 134-35. Captain Fuller, a seasoned veteran of waterborn battles, was in charge of General Taylor's small fleet of gunboats. Banks to Halleck, April 17, 1863, *OR*, Series 1, vol. 20, p. 139.

24. Farragut to Alden, April 23, 1863, *ORN*, Series 1, vol. 20, pp. 62-63. *ORN*, Series 1, vol. 19, pp. 523-25, citing *Houston Tri-Weekly Telegraph*, February 2, 1863. Benjamin to Seddon, December 3, 1862, *ORN*, Series 1, vol. 19, pp. 334-37.

25. Feelings of respect, if not admiration, may be inferred from remarks of a Federal seaman on board the *Calhoun*, who recorded in his diary, "This was a remarkable battle. The captain of the Queen was named Fuller; he had commanded the J. A. Cotton in all of her fights against us. He was quoted as saying: "There is that d---- Calhoun. I would rather see the devil than that boat." Extract, diary of Acting Third Assistant Engineer George W. Baird, U.S. Navy, U.S.S. *Calhoun*, April 14,.1863, *ORN*, Series 1, vol. 20, pp. 137-38. One Northern newspaper said of Fuller, "he is evidently a plebeian—that is, not an F.F. [first families]—a man of strong native sense, believes in State rights, and that the cause of the South is more just and sacred than that of the Colonies in the American Revolution, and is to-day a very fair representative of that class who two years since were opposed to secession. His personal bravery is well attested, and he bears on and in his own person many a certificate of presence in well-fought fields." *New York Daily Tribune*, June 11, 1863.

26. National Archives and Records Administration (NARA) Washington, D.C., War Department Collection of Compiled Service Records (CSR) of Confederate Soldiers Who Served During the Civil War. Records of Captain Julius Giesecke, 4th Texas Cavalry, Records Group (RG) 109. *CMH*, vol. 15, *Texas*, by Oran M. Roberts, pp. 418-19. Sibley to Cooper, February 22, 1862, *OR*, Series 1, vol. 9, pp. 505-518.

27. Richard Taylor, *Destruction and Reconstruction: Personal Experiences of the Late War* (New York: D. Appleton and Company, 1879) p. 109. Taylor to Boggs, April 23, 1863, *OR*, Series 1, vol. 15, p. 396.

28. *New York Times*, June 14, June 30, and July 15, 1856; June 29, 1857. John Myers Myers, *San Francisco's Reign of Terror* (Garden City, NY: Doubleday & Company, 1966), p. 252-56. Reportedly, the deceased, James King, added to his name the suffix, "of William," to indicate that he was the son of William, thereby distinguishing himself from others named James King. During his journey into Mexico, McGowan and his son accompanied Charles P. Stone, who would later be responsible for the initial defenses of Washington, and be imprisoned without charges for six months after being blamed for the Union defeat at Ball's Bluff.

29. Banks to Grant, April 23, 1863, *OR*, Series 1, vol. 15, p. 303. The tone of General Banks' letter conveys his great excitement at the day's success regarding the naval vessels destroyed, notwithstanding that he had failed in his primary objective to defeat or capture General Taylor's army at Irish Bend, a failure that would come back to haunt him when he again met Taylor the following year.

30. *CMH*, vol. 2, *Maryland*, by Bradley T. Johnson, pp. 266-69.

31. NARA, CSR of Allen Rufus Witt, 10th Ark. Inf., RG 109. A native of Quitman, Arkansas, by the time the war began, Witt had attended college, travelled to California with a cattle drive, and served as state land commissioner. He was elected commander of the 10th Arkansas shortly after the battle of Shiloh, in which he was wounded while serving as commander of Company A. *Biographical and Historical Memoirs of Central Arkansas* (Chicago, Nashville, and St. Louis: The Goodspeed Publishing Co., 1889; repr., Easley, S.C.: Southern Historical Press, 1978), pp. 744-45. See also, David C. Edmonds, *The Guns of Port Hudson*, vol. 2, *The Investment, Siege and Reduction* (Lafayette, La.: The Arcadia Press, 1984), p. 43.

32. Began in 1819, work on Fort Monroe continued up to the eve of the war, though it was essentially completed by the mid-thirties. Richard P. Weinert, Jr., and Colonel Robert Arthur, *Defender of the Chesapeake - The Story of Fort Monroe* (Annapolis, Md.: Leeward Publications, Inc., 1978), pp. 20-36.

33. Haas, "Diary of Julius Giesecke," p. 30.

34. Morris, *History of the Sixth New York Zouaves*, pp. 142-43. Wilson's treatment of the Confederate officers is even more remarkable considering that the *Cahawba* was carrying home the bodies of the commanders of the 116th and 128th New York Infantry, *New York Herald*, June 9, 1863.

35. Heyl, *Early American Steamers*, vol. 5, pp. 283-84.

36. Originally of Canadian registry, the vessel was purchased by American interests at the beginning of the war and the Federal government chartered it for use as a transport. The vessel had three decks, and measured 173 feet in length. Heyl, *Early American Steamers*, vol. 5, pp. 171-75.

37. Bowen to Dix, June 2, 1863, *OR*, Series 2, vol. 5, p. 730. Jefferson Davis's proclamation of December 23, 1862, was published in General Order 111, December 24, 1862. See *OR*, Series 2, vol. 5, pp. 795-7. For a discussion of this episode, and the Southern reaction to recruiting black troops, see Dudley Taylor Cornish, *The Sable Arm, Black Troops in the Union Army, 1861-1865* (Lawrence, Kans.: University Press of Kansas, 1987), pp. 158-63.

38. Asbury, *My Experiences in the War*, p. 19.

39. Haas, "Diary of Julius Giesecke," pp. 30-34.

40. The grades referred to in the text, and the accompanying roster, are those the individuals held in June of 1863, even though later they may have changed.

41. John B. Wolf, "Capture of the Maple Leaf," *Confederate Veteran* 6 (August 1898): 386. *Washington Evening Star*, June 13, 1863.

42. Camp Hamilton was located just across Mill Creek, which separates Fort Monroe from Hampton, Virginia. Weinert, *Defender of the Chesapeake*, p. 87.

43. Special Order Number 159, Headquarters, Department of Virginia, VII Army Corps, Fort Monroe, Virginia, June 9, 1863, directed:
> Lieut. Wm. Dorsey, 3' Regt Pa Arty will proceed in charge of certain Prisoners of War in the Steamer Maple Leaf to Fort Norfolk, Va., there to take on more Prisoners of War. He will then proceed with the same steamer to Fort Delaware, Del. and transfer the prisoners to the Cmdg Officer of that Post, taking his receipt, and then returning with the Steamer and report to this Headquarters.

NARA, Records of the Adjutant General's Office, Department of War, RG 94.

Chapter 2

Rising on the Guard

The skipper of the *Maple Leaf* was Captain Henry W. Dale. The ship's other officers were W. A. Smith, engineer; John Carmine, pilot; and Charles H. Farnham, mate. The size of the crew, all black, is uncertain. It has been claimed that they numbered as many as fifty, but it was probably closer to thirty.[1]

As long as there was hope for exchange or parole, the men of the New Orleans group were content to wait and watch. Once on board the *Maple Leaf* and sailing for prison at Fort Delaware, however, Captain Fuller quickly devised a plan of escape and organized its execution. Other leaders of the plot were Captains Semmes, Holmes, and Colonel Witt.[2]

Some of the officers who had been confined at Fort Norfolk felt that they had been mistreated. This was particularly true of Colonel Green and his companions, who had travelled from St. Louis to Fort Norfolk under parole to cooperate with their captors. They believed that the conditions of their confinement at Fort Norfolk were far from the lenient treatment promised in St. Louis. When they learned that several of the prisoners from New Orleans were plotting an escape, they were ready to join the attempt.

One of the Confederates later wrote, "a fairly vigilant watch was kept up by the Federals while we were in port and until we got out to sea; but once safely away from shore, they relaxed their vigilance, trusting to the water and our submission to fate."[3] The prisoners were allowed to roam about the ship, conversing with each other and with the guards. This freedom to move about was of great help to those plotting the escape, since their plan called for several Confederates to overwhelm each sentry at a given signal, the ringing of the ship's bell.[4] At least one of the Rebel officers managed to gain admission to the pilot house, within reach of the bell, for this purpose. Confederate Captain John B. Wolf later identified this individual as Captain Eugene Holmes of Louisiana's Crescent Regiment.[5]

The ship not long out of sight of Fort Monroe, having been under way for about two hours, "and at a point approximately six miles north of Cape Henry Light House,"[6] when above the steady churning of the ship's engines, the Confederates heard the ringing of the ship's bell calling them to action. They quickly overwhelmed the sentries, and seized their rifles. Captain Seckel states that after agreeing to take part in the uprising, he was told to watch a particular sentry, and upon hearing three "taps" of the ships' bell, to seize the man's musket. He went on to relate that he "had that musket at the first tap."[7]

According to Captain Morse, the Confederates decided to make their move at about 5:30 P.M., while there was still light, and to avoid the danger of the plot being discovered if they waited longer.

With the guard easily subdued, the now-armed Confederates had control of the *Maple Leaf*. According to one of the prisoners, "the Confederate 'yell' rang out that evening upon the Chesapeake as it never will again," and there was a "rousing demonstration." The Confederates were now in a joyful mood, and "a fusillade of jokes and bantering" ensued. The single casualty of the episode was a sentry who briefly resisted, and who was struck down with his own musket, but without serious injury.[8]

Captain Asbury, who was sick in the hold of the ship, related that "grey uniforms took the place of blue, the vessel moved on as if nothing had occurred; the course was varied a little, a hurried council was held, and the captain of the 'Star of the West' [*sic*] took command of the Maple Leaf."[9]

Captain Morse related that some of the men found the ship's pantry and bar. The result was a fine dinner, but too much drinking, and the guard watching over the Yankee soldiers was charged with securing the liquor stores as well.

Some of the Confederates were in favor of taking the ship to the British colony of Nassau, some two hundred miles east of Key Largo, Florida. However, Captain Dale told them that there was not enough coal on board for such a trip.[10] Besides, the area was known to be infested with Union vessels enforcing the blockade of Southern ports, and the notion was voted down. Because of his experience with Confederate gunboats, and despite his injuries, the

31

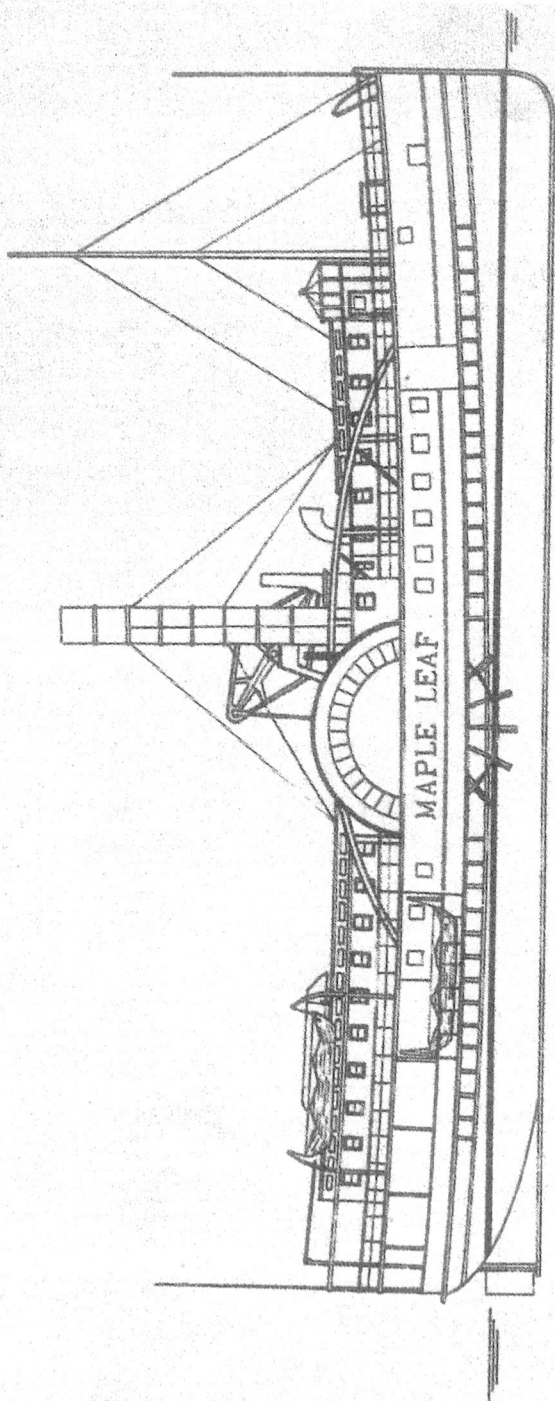

Rebels chose Captain Fuller as their skipper. They were unable, however, to persuade him to join in the escape.[11]

The Rebels had observed Federal gunboats while the *Maple Leaf* was still in Hampton Roads, and although they would soon enjoy the protection of darkness, it was important that they leave the ship before any naval vessel became suspicious. The ship rounded Cape Henry, and proceeded south, running along the Virginia coast to a point some ten to fifteen miles from Cape Henry[12] and a half-mile from shore. There they stopped the engine, and the Confederates began their preparations to leave the ship.[13]

The Rebels were not unanimous in their desire to escape. This was particularly true of some of those who had promised back in St. Louis that they would cooperate with their captors. Technically, one of the possible penalties for violation of parole was death,[14] and there was a good likelihood of their being recaptured. Further, the trip back to Confederate lines would involve a long journey on foot, a portion of which would be through at least the periphery of the massive Dismal Swamp. Twenty-seven of the men chose to remain with the *Maple Leaf*, even though it meant returning to Federal custody. Several of them—Green states twelve to fifteen were sick or wounded—were incapable of walking a long distance. (See annotations on the roster at Appendix A.)

Among those of the Fort Norfolk Group who had travelled from St. Louis, there was lively debate regarding the "paroles" they had given before leaving the Gratiot Street Prison. Most argued that their promises of cooperation with Union authorities were conditioned on lenient treatment—promises the Yankees had cancelled by the harsh conditions imposed at Fort Norfolk. A few, however, insisted that their oaths remained in effect, and vowed to stick by them. The majority accused those who were fit to travel, but who chose not to escape only because of their "paroles," of having excessively delicate consciences, and worse, of harboring devious motives with intent to avoid further service to the Confederacy; they derisively referred to those in this group as "conscience men."[15]

The members of the New Orleans Group were under no obligation to their captors, however, and should have been expected

On board the "Maple Leaf"
June the 10th 1863

I William E Laisey
Lieut N.S.A. do solemnly
swear that I will pursue
my contemplated trip
from Fortress Munroe
to Fort Delaware
without stopping at any
point or giving any
information concerning
this day's transaction
on board the steamer
"Maple Leaf" until
my arrival at
Fort Delaware

Sworn to and subscribed
before me on board
the S.S. Maple Leaf   W E Bowley
June 10th.63.   Lt 5 Per Ark

Commanding Guard Steamer
F. Case

to attempt an escape whenever possible, since it was their obligation to do so. Four of this number, including Captain Fuller, remained with the ship because of injuries which made them unfit for a long journey. (Two of the four died within the next six months.)

As soon as they realized the probability that Captain Fuller would have to remain with the ship, and would thus fall back into Federal hands, the plotters devised a scheme to draw blame away from him by making it appear that the leader of the plot was Edward McGowan, who had gained a reputation—from his San Francisco days and earlier—for daring exploits, and who had convinced the Yankees that he was the former purser of the *Diana*.

The seventy officers who chose to go ahead with the escape knew that there was a greater chance they would be recaptured if the matter was promptly reported to the Yankees. To prevent this, they would have scuttled the *Maple Leaf* but for their concern for their fellow officers who remained on board.[16] Then they conceived the novel, though somewhat naive, notion of requiring Lieutenant Dorsey and the ship's officers to give their own paroles; that is, their promises that they would proceed directly to Fort Delaware, and not report the escape until they arrived at that destination. They obtained from Lieutenant Dorsey, and Captain Dale, the following promise:[17]

On board the "Maple Leaf"
June the 10th 1863

I William E. Dorsey, Lieut., U.S.A., do solemnly swear that I will pursue my contemplated trip from Fortress Monroe to Fort Delaware without stopping at any point or giving any information concerning this day's transaction on board the steamer "Maple Leaf" until my arrival at Fort Delaware.

Sworn to and subscribed	W. E. Dorsey
before me on board the	Lt, 3d Penn. Arty.
Str Maple Leaf	Cmdg Steamer
June 10, 1863	
Edward McGowan	
Lt Cmdg	

The Rebels had McGowan witness these "paroles" of Dale and Dorsey, signing as "Lt Cmdg" (Lieutenant, Commanding) in order to bolster the chance of convincing the Yankees that he was the leader of the plot to seize the ship, thereby drawing some suspicion away from Fuller—even though Fuller had already been introduced to Captain Dale as the "new captain of the Maple Leaf." Nevertheless, the scheme met with a degree of success. It was later reported to General Dix and to the public by several newspapers that the escape was planned and led by Lieutenant McGowan.[18]

As a gesture of good will toward the unfortunate Lieutenant, and at his request, the Confederate officers gave Dorsey the following note, intended to shield him from suspicion of conniving with the Rebels.[19]

> *Confederate States (late United States) Transport,*
> *"Maple Leaf"*
> *At Sea, June 10, 1863*
> Major-General Dix, *Commanding Fortress Monroe and adjoining District:*
> *General:* - We, the undersigned officers of the Confederate States, while being held as prisoners of war, did forcibly seize and take possession of steamer *Maple Leaf*, guard and crew.
> Lately yours, with regret,
> (Signed by the principal actors in the attack)

Feeling that they had done as much as they could to protect Fuller and hoping that their escape would not be known to Union forces until they were well on their way to safety, the group made its way to shore by means of several trips in the small boats carried aboard the ship. They completed their landing at about sundown.[20]

With the departure of the last of the escaping Confederates, Captain Dale regained control of the *Maple Leaf*. He promptly ordered Captain Fuller confined to a stateroom, and lost no time in getting the ship underway, its great wheels again churning the water as it swung north toward Fort Delaware.[21]

Notes

1. Green, *Life in Prison and Escape*, p. 27. The crew is known to have numbered thirty-one in March 1864.

2. A. E. Asbury, "Capture of the Maple Leaf," *Confederate Veteran* 6 (November 1898): 529. J. Thomas Scharf, *History of the Confederate States Navy* (New York: Rogers & Sherwood, 1887), pp. 721-22. Speaking of Captain Fuller, Green states that shortly after boarding the *Maple Leaf*, "a low bulky, heavy set man with iron gray hair was pointed out as captain, whose orders were to be obeyed implicitly." Green *Life in Prison and Escape*, p. 27. Several of the conspirators (Fuller, Holmes, Semmes and Witt) were among those who, two days earlier, presented a formal resolution to their guard on the *Cahawba* memorializing their appreciation for "kind and courteous treatment."

3. Wolf, "Capture of the Maple Leaf," p. 375.

4. Green, *Life in Prison and Escape*, p. 27. Some of the Confederate officers, notably Alston and Wolf, later claimed that liquor, a large dinner, and the resulting "mellowing" of Lt. Dorsey, played some role in the affair. However, the most detailed accounts make no mention of the matter. *CMH*, vol. 13, *Louisiana*, by John Dimitry, p. 326, and vol. 15, *Texas*, by O. M. Roberts, pp. 704-05.

5. Wolf, "Capture of the Maple Leaf," 375. In a later statement, Captain Dale omitted any reference to the ship's bell, claiming only, "I heard a slight noise below, when one of the crew ran up and informed me the guards were fighting, and almost immediately several officers appeared on deck, with our soldiers' guns, and said the boat was under their charge and control and a man called by name Capt. Fuller, had then command of the boat." *Boston Daily Advertiser*, June 15, 1863.

6. NARA, Ludlow to Dix, June 12, 1863, RG 94.

7. Yeary, *Reminiscences of the Boys in Gray*, p. 674.

8. Green, *Life in Prison and Escape*, p. 28. Asbury, "Capture of the Maple Leaf," p. 529. Wolf, "Capture of the Maple Leaf," p. 375.

9. Asbury, *My Experiences*, p. 20.

10. Ludlow to Dix, June 12, 1863.

11. A. F. Wilson, "Would Not Surrender the Flag - Reminiscences of the Queen of the West," *Confederate Veteran*, 10 (February 1902): 72. Asbury, "Capture of the Maple Leaf," p. 529. Green, *Life in Prison and Escape*, p. 28. Fuller had been released from a Federal hospital some three weeks earlier with wounds to both arms, and a fracture of his right. Andrew B. Booth, comp., *Records of Louisiana Confederate Soldiers and Louisiana Confederate Commands* (New Orleans: 1920.)

12. An inquiry later concluded, based in part on information gained from Confederates—who would not have hesitated to mislead the investigating officer—that the prisoners left the ship some eight miles south of Cape Henry, an estimate concurred in by Captain Dale. Other reports say the *Maple Leaf* was as much as forty-five miles south of Cape Henry when the Confederates left the ship.

13. Asbury, "Capture of the Maple Leaf," p. 529.

14. William Winthrop, *Military Law and Precedents*, War Department Document 1001 (Washington, D.C.: GPO, 1886; repr., 1920), p. 793. Although the death penalty could be imposed for a violation of parole given pursuant to the cartel it was not contemplated for violation of the informal paroles discussed here. However, it is not likely that the Rebel officers were aware of the legal distinction, and neither, it would later appear, was Colonel Ludlow, the Federal Commissioner of Exchange. See note 2, Chapter 4.

15. Green, *Life in Prison and Escape*, p. 31.

16. *Daily Richmond Examiner*, June 23, 1863.

17. NARA, CSR of William E. Dorsey, 3d Pennsylvania Artillery, RG 94. NARA, Ludlow to Dix, June 12, 1863, National Archives, RG 94.

18. "The man who led [the Rebels] is no less than the notorious Judge McGowan of San Francisco Vigilance Committee popularity." *Philadelphia Inquirer*, June 15, 1863.

19. Morse, "The Capture of the 'Maple Leaf'," p. 306

20. Wolf, "Capture of the Maple Leaf," 375. Captain Dale estimated that the landings were completed about 8:30 P.M. *Boston Daily Advertiser*, June 15, 1863.

21. Though it apparently did not hinder his later navigation of the *Maple Leaf*, Captain Dale later reported that before the Confederates left the ship, they cut a large piece out of his chart for use in guiding them through unfamiliar country. *Philadelphia Inquirer*, June 15, 1863.

Chapter 3

I Hove Up for Fortress Monroe

Soon after the fleeing Rebels left the *Maple Leaf* and the ship got under way, Lieutenant Dorsey and Captain Dale reconsidered their position, and decided—or perhaps they had intended all along—to return to Fort Monroe and report the escape, disregarding the oaths taken only a short while earlier promising to proceed to Fort Delaware. Upon reaching Cape Henry, Captain Dale states that he "hove up for Fortress Monroe."[1]

The *Maple Leaf* returned to the mouth of Hampton Roads near midnight.[2] With seventy of her prisoners missing, and Dorsey's guard detail disarmed, her sudden appearance in the middle of the night was a disturbing surprise to the few of Fort Monroe's garrison who were up to greet her and who anxiously sought to learn from Dorsey and Dale what had happened.

Captain Fuller's brief time as "captain" of the *Maple Leaf* were sufficient to earn him the angry wrath of the Yankees, even though they did not suspect the full extent of his involvement. He was placed in irons, and with the others who remained with the ship, were subjected to "very severe treatment."[3]

Lieutenant Dorsey delayed the disagreeable task of informing the responsible officials of the escape until around nine o'clock the next morning.[4] It was only then that he reported the matter to Lieutenant Colonel William H. Ludlow, assistant inspector general and Federal agent for exchange of prisoners of war. General Dix was away from Fort Monroe, having departed the previous day aboard the *C. W. Thomas* for a visit to Williamsburg. Acting for Dix, Ludlow promptly took steps to recapture the fleeing Confederates, measures which might have been taken hours earlier with greater effect. He telegraphed messages to the Federal commanders at Suffolk and Norfolk, ordering that cavalry be sent in pursuit.[5]

On the afternoon of June 11, Dix returned to Fort Monroe to receive the disturbing news of the escape. At four o'clock he dispatched a message to the Union Army's general-in-chief, Major General Henry W. Halleck:

> I have just returned from Williamsburg, where I went at 10 o'clock yesterday morning. At 1:30 the Maple Leaf left for Fort Delaware, with 97 rebel officers. They rose on the guard, overpowered it, took possession of the steamer, and landed below Cape Henry. Thirty [sic] of the officers refused to participate in the transaction, remained on board, and are here. Our cavalry is in pursuit of the others.
>
> The Officer in charge of the guard was grossly negligent, and should be dismissed the service.
>
> Lieutenant-Colonel [B.C.] [sic] Ludlow will make a detailed report, which I will forward tomorrow.[6]

The sudden return of the *Maple Leaf* attracted a lot of attention. Reporters for Northern newspapers seized on the escape story, and by that weekend articles describing the incident appeared in the papers of several Northern cities, including New York, Boston, Philadelphia, and Washington.[7] Some were very critical of Federal handling of the matter, one paper claiming:

> If these prisoners did not give their parole, their escape was most disgraceful to the guard . . . or to the Federal authorities for furnishing a guard not strong enough . . . . ' Tis scandalous, that . . . rebel officers, captured at a heavy cost of toil and blood, are allowed to slip lightly through our fingers.[8]

Typically, the leadership of the two armies disagreed on the right of the prisoners to escape. General Dix took the position that the "paroles" given by the Confederate officers of the Fort Norfolk Group were valid, and that some of those officers honorably kept their word; on the other hand, Confederate Secretary of War James A. Seddon claimed that the paroles had been invalidated by mistreatment of the prisoners, and that those who remained with the ship only did so because they were unable to travel. Both men were right with regard to a portion of the prisoners. Some of the Fort Norfolk Group remained because they were unable to travel. Others of the group remained because of the obligation they felt to honor their promises. Officials on both sides of the issue seemed to disregard the fact that the majority of prisoners were not subject to the claimed paroles.

Some of the Confederates who remained on board the *Maple Leaf*, and were now in close arrest, attempted to see Colonel Ludlow, probably to protest their treatment. To their way of thinking, they had proven that their confinement was unnecessary and they could be trusted, as demonstrated by their refusing to escape when they had the opportunity. It does not appear, however, that their request for an interview was granted.[9]

On June 11, Colonel Ludlow conducted a brief investigation into the cause of the escape, and made his report to General Dix, concluding erroneously, as the Rebels had intended him to, that the plot was led by Lieutenant McGowan. (See Appendix C.) The next day, Friday, June 12, 1863, the *Maple Leaf* sailed from Fort Monroe for the third time in four days, proceeding to deliver the twenty-seven remaining prisoners to Fort Delaware, this time, with a different commander of the guard.

Notes

1. Boston Daily Advertiser, June 15, 1863. Dale likely had mixed emotions about the day's events. He was probably disgusted at the loss of the prisoners, and the inadequate guard provided, but relieved that his ship was saved.

2. Ludlow to Dix, June 12, 1863. See also Asbury, "Capture of the Maple Leaf", p. 529.

3. Confederate Veteran, "My Experiences in the War of 1861-65," 20 (May 1912): 242.

4. *New York Daily Tribune*, June 12, 1862 (byline Fort Monroe, June 10, 1863). This report, which includes several known errors, quotes Captain Dale as claiming that Dorsey reported the escape immediately upon the return of the *Maple Leaf* to Fort Monroe, a reasonable assumption—and what should have happened, but did not. *Boston Daily Advertiser*, June 15, 1863.

5. Ludlow to Dix, June 12, 1863.

6. Dix to Halleck, June 11, 1863, *OR*, Series 1, vol. 27, pt. 2, p. 786. A phrase from this letter was often repeated afterwards, and included in a notation made in the file of each of the seventy officers who escaped: "This man was one of the prisoners of war who, on June 10, 1863, while being transported from Fortress Monroe, Va., to Fort Delaware, Del. on the Steamer Maple Leaf, rose on the guard, overpowered it and made their escape."

7. *Washington Evening Star*, June 13, 1863. See also, *New York Times*, June 14, 1863, and *Philadelphia Inquirer*, June 15, 1863.

8. *San Francisco Alta California*, 13 July 1863, quoting the *Louisville Journal*.

9. NARA, Lynn and Francis to Ludlow, June 12, 1863, RG 109. The complete note is as follows:

> St Boat Maple Leaf
> Off Fortress Monroe
> June 12 1863
>
> Col. Ludlow
> Sir--We have represented our cases _indirectly_ to you several times, but it has been attended with _no_ satisfaction to us, and now we desire to communicate _directly_ with you and ask that you favor us with an interview before we leave.
> -Very Resp'fly
> D. Lynne
> Capt, Co B, 19th Va Regt
> Thomas H. Francis
> Capt, Co A, 4th Reg't T.V.

Chapter 4

The Federal Army in Their Front

The small boats from the *Maple Leaf* brought the Rebels to shore on the Outer Banks in Princess Anne County, Virginia, not far from its border with North Carolina. (See map, page 47.) Once on land, the Confederates faced several obstacles to an overland journey to Richmond: specifically, Currituck Sound (which separates the Outer Banks from the mainland), some two hundred miles of woodland, several rivers, and Dismal Swamp. Added to their problems, were some that they were not yet aware of but would soon learn: they were still within Union lines,[1] Yankee cavalry was pursuing them, and some Federal officials believed that, if caught, the Rebels should be summarily executed.[2]

Lieutenant Colonel Ludlow's message, alerting Union cavalry to the escape and ordering them to intercept the fugitives, received a prompt response from the Yankee outpost at Suffolk, Virginia, where the colorful Brigadier General Michael Corcoran of New York was in command of the First Division of the Seventh Corps. As fiercely Irish as he was pro-Union, at the outbreak of the war Corcoran was awaiting court-martial for refusing to lead his regiment, the 69th New York Militia, in a parade honoring the visiting Prince of Wales. With the start of war the disciplinary proceedings were put aside, however, and he entered Federal service with his regiment. Captured while leading his men at First Bull Run, the Confederates held Corcoran for thirteen months before exchanging him in August of 1862.[3]

At the time the Suffolk garrison was alerted to intercept the Rebels from the *Maple Leaf*, Corcoran was smarting from the results of a tragic incident in which he had killed another Union officer, one Lieutenant Colonel Edwin A. Kimball, an acting regimental commander and a hero of several battles, including Antietam. Kimball had unquestionably provoked the incident, but at the time he was also scandalously drunk.[4] Kimball's regiment was outraged, some say ready to mutiny.[5]

For General Corcoran, his troops' recapture of the Rebels from the *Maple Leaf* would inject a positive and very welcome note to his reputation. One of those he sent in pursuit of the fleeing Confederates was Major James N. Wheelan,[6] who was commanding several companies of the 7th New York Cavalry on duty at nearby South Mills, North Carolina. Wheelan's troops promptly began vigorous patrolling in search of the Confederates.

As for the Confederates, as soon as they reached the Virginia shore, they elected Captain Semmes—likely the only one of the group with substantial military training—their leader. Captain Eugene Holmes, of Louisiana's Crescent Regiment, was chosen as second in command. At the time, "about all they knew was that they had the Atlantic Ocean in their rear and the Federal Army in their front."[7]

The Rebels then had the good fortune to come upon a woman whose husband was away in the Confederate Army. It was she who told them that they were in Princess Anne County. She also gave them advice on how they might make their way across Currituck Sound, and into the vicinity of Dismal Swamp, where they should try to contact a company of North Carolina home guards, commanded by Captain Willis Sanderlin. She even allowed them to borrow her cart and horse, surely aware of the risk of its being taken or destroyed by Federal patrols.[8]

With only a loosely formed notion of getting help from Sanderlin, the unwieldy column of seventy men set out that evening marching south in single file along the shore. All of the men suffered from lack of water that night. Some, many of them cavalrymen, had rough going because they were not accustomed to travelling on foot. Captain Morse spoke of walking in the heat and heavy sand, the men filling their mouths with tobacco or bullets in an effort to relieve their thirst. Colonel Green endured great pain because he was wearing new boots, purchased just as he left St. Louis only five days earlier. He took them off, but the rough sand soon shredded his stockings, and then the soles of his feet "were worn through by the hard and gritty track." Once he approached the cart at the head of the column with the thought of riding a spell for relief from the pain of walking. He found, however, that all space was taken by men in worse condition than

Michael Corcoran

himself. Describing the first time he had witnessed the sun rising from the sea, Green later wrote of the dawn of June 11, that "tongues of flame shot up out of the water at first, and then the great burning globe leaped out of the water as if an invisible hand had lifted it suddenly out of the sea." Soon afterward, suffering from thirst and exhaustion, he temporarily lost consciousness.[9]

Shortly after dawn the Rebel column came upon the camp of a small group of men who were boiling sea water to make salt. Fresh water was available, and the officers rested and refreshed themselves throughout the day. That evening, using the salt makers' open sailboats, they made a turbulent crossing of Currituck Sound amid high winds and rough seas. Soaked and chilled to the bone, it was near midnight when they reached the mainland. There they built fires to warm themselves and dry their clothes. Then they slept until dawn.[10]

On the next day, June 12, the Rebels encountered a second woman also married to a Confederate soldier. She agreed to help them locate Captain Sanderlin's men, and then left to find one of her neighbors to help her prepare breakfast for the group. A short while later she came running back to where the Rebels were resting. Out of breath, she told them that a regiment of Yankee cavalry had just passed near the front gate of her property. After waiting a while to make certain that the Yankee horsemen were no longer about, the Rebels resumed marching, now at a high state of alert. They soon entered the swamp,[11] and waited there for several hours. Eventually, one of their number who had been posted as a sentinel appeared, accompanied by a man in civilian dress. The stranger carried a shotgun and had two pistols in his belt. It was Sanderlin.

The company of home guards led by Captain Willis Burgess Sanderlin, age thirty-two, consisted of some fifty-five men. For many months they had harassed Federal forces in guerrilla actions, and were themselves the quarry of Federal expeditions seeking their capture or destruction.

With Sanderlin guiding them, the group set out toward Elizabeth City. Again they marched in single file, and, to avoid detection, traveled only at night, sometimes finding their way in the darkness only by forming a human chain, with each man holding the shirt tail or belt of the man in front of him. The ground

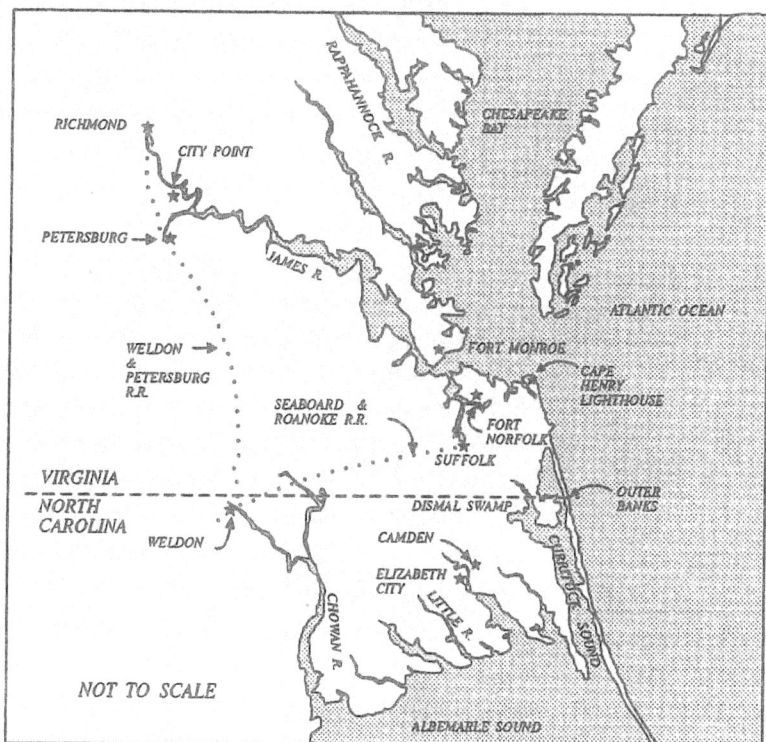

Some key features of the vicinity of the escape.

was covered with moss, vegetation and mold, which softened the sound of their own marching, but at the same time, muffled the noise of hoof beats, which they relied upon to warn them of the approach of Union cavalry. They quickly learned to listen for the faintest clinking of sabres or spurs, a sure sign that the horsemen were about. The first to detect their presence would give the alarm, a low whistle, or desperately whisper the warning, "saber! saber!"[12]

Captain Morse described a night in the swamp:

> Listened last night to the adventures and escapes of an old Californian (Judge McGowan), whose chequered career and hair-breadth escapes would fill a volume; we are encouraged by his tones and profit by his experience. The stars shine brightly, but the dew falls like rain, and we drop asleep, tired, exhausted, and shivering with cold.

The goal of the wary band was to cross the Pasquotank River near Elizabeth City using boats that the Home Guard had sunk earlier to prevent their discovery and destruction by Union patrols. Their planned route would take them through the vicinity of Camden Court House and Elizabeth City toward the Chowan River further west.

Colonel Green related an incident which occurred one evening while the men were waiting for a delivery of rations near Camden Court House, just a few miles from Elizabeth City. Watching near a road, he was surprised at the approach of a large number of wagons and carts, many of them carrying women bringing food. They said that it had been more than a year since they had seen Confederate uniforms, and had come to look at them once more.

> We met and talked with all the freedom of old friends who had met after a long separation. A dance was proposed and, but for the lack of a fiddle, our company would have taken all the chances of capture for one hour's dance in Dismal Swamp with the Camden girls. Knowing that we would be going through their town by night, they stayed and made the night's march with us.[13]

Similarly, an account of the experiences of Captain Edward Parker describes his journey assisted and protected by the local residents, "as loyal, big-hearted people as live upon this earth, and they were by them concealed by day in the dense forests and piloted by night in short states in the direction of the Confederate lines. . . . Even the ladies came into the deep woods to bring cheer and food to the hunted as they bivouacked under the moss-draped trees of swamp and woodland."[14]

Another of the rare accounts of the journey was provided by Captain Seckel, who must have often thought of the adventure in later years. In its partly irrelevant entirety, it goes:

> While in the dismal swamps, after we had proven who we were, a young lady, Miss Adelaide Campbell, brought us a pound cake with a Confederate flag stuck in the center, and you bet we gave her three cheers three times over. She was a daughter of the sunny South, lovely, pure and true. I hope she still lives, and I know that if she does not she is in Paradise.[15]

Somewhere in the vicinity of Camden Court House, Semmes and the other Rebel leaders decided that they should divide the awkwardly maneuvered column into three smaller, more manageable groups.[16] There were still several rivers to cross and many miles to travel through country seemingly filled with Yankee patrols. Giesecke recorded in his diary that on one occasion, "the Yankee pickets were posted so near around us that it was impossible for even Captain Sandley [sic] to pass their lines and come to us . . . with . . . provisions."[17]

When the group that included Colonel Green reached the Chowan River, they found that their intended crossing point was blocked by a Federal gunboat. Their guide, a young boy, persuaded one of the local citizens to send a message to the commander of the gunboat, reporting that the escaped prisoners were attempting to cross the river further upstream. The gunboat quickly left. The guide then returned with a blind man who took the party of fugitives across the river. Col. Green described him as "large, robust, bushy headed, long-bearded, and old enough for his hair and beard to be as white as snow. We named him Charon, he having all the feature of his ancient predecessor . . . except the charging of an obolus for the passage. This blind old Charon would not have one cent, though we showed him the money and begged him to take it."[18]

On the west bank of the Chowan, the party spent the night at a house near the landing. The owner stated that he had promised not to aid the rebels, but that "if they made him furnish supper, lodging, and breakfast, and even compelled him to get out an old demijohn of whiskey, he couldn't help it."[19]

The next morning Green and his companions were taken by wagon across the remaining twenty-five miles of what he termed "disputed territory," eventually coming upon the tracks of the Seaboard & Roanoke Railroad. The other groups found the railway at other places along the line, but at about the same time. Colonel Dougherty and Captain Seckel, traveling on their own, managed to find the railway and transportation to Richmond several days ahead of the main body.[20]

The escaping officers received substantial aid from Captain Sanderlin and his company of Home Guards,[21] but also from many members of the civilian communities through which they passed. Recorded tradition in Camden County tells, with minor discrepancies, of the efforts of one Wealthy Burgess, a sister of one of Captain Sanderlin's men, to assist the Southern officers from the *Maple Leaf*. According to the story, because it was believed that a woman would be more successful at passing the Yankee patrols, Wealthy Burgess volunteered to act as guide for a group of the Confederates. Avoiding the roads, she walked eight miles through the swampy forest to meet the waiting officers, then returned with them, leading them to a boat which transported them safely away in the night.[22]

The Rebel officers may not have fully realized their impact on the country dwellers and small villages such as Camden Court House. Their mere presence, in the face of pursuing Federal Cavalry, would have been disturbing enough. Added to that, however, was the obligation the people felt to protect and assist their fleeing countrymen. Feeding seventy men a single meal was surely difficult for the sparsely settled community of farmers; supporting them for several days must have been severely taxing. Yet help for the Rebels was never lacking, and several veterans later wrote of the "good people of North Carolina."[23]

Julius Giesecke told of one community which held a brief religious service, praying for the safety of the Rebel officers. In his entry for Saturday, June 20, 1863, he states:

> We went about four miles when we arrived at Church Bethel in Showan [Chowan] County where we were kindly treated by the people of the place. We were asked to first attend a short service and then were furnished wagons to transport us the balance of twelve miles to the ferry on Showan River and we were also provided with ample supply of cake and victuals. Shortly before night we left the church and those good people and at midnight arrived at the ferry.[24]

Morse apparently was describing the same event when he wrote:

> At 4 o'clock yesterday evening reached Bethel Church (a modest place of worship in the midst of the forest), where all the women of the neighborhood waited to receive us. Many brought provisions, delicacies, and flowers, and the more prudent old farmers dispensed most excellent peach brandy to the faint and weary. After partaking of the substantials and liquids we entered the church, sang a hymn and prayed; and the hearts of all present went up to God in honest thanksgiving and praise from that low-roofed chapel in the wild woods.

The gathering at Church Bethel described by Giesecke and Morse may have been the same one attended by Parthenia Gatling when a girl of fourteen. Writing of the event in 1899, she recalled that in June of 1863, her family lived between Edenton and Hertford, just east of the Chowan River. She had come home from the Hertford Academy for the week-end, bringing along two friends and a "lady teacher." On Saturday, Captain Whitaker Myers of the local militia[25] called at her house to tell her father that one of the Confederate bands from the *Maple Leaf* would be passing in the vicinity of nearby Bethel Church, and to ask for his help in feeding them. She went on to relate:

> My father told the captain that he would do what he could with pleasure—quite a number of others in the neighborhood had acceded to the same request from the captain. My mother put all the cooks to cooking as fast as possible, and . . . suggested that all of us should go to the church to see those brave Confederates, and wish them a safe journey to their friends and comrades.
>
> The lady teacher, the school girls and myself were delighted with the idea of seeing some real soldiers in their uniforms, and gathered flowers to take to them . . . . My father laughed at us and said that those hungry, tired men would not care for flowers, but only for the provision in the big basket that was in the cart.

Speaking of their meeting with the Confederates that evening, she continued:

> The whole family went after an early dinner to the church ground, and there they saw, the wonderful "Maple Leaf" captors . . . assembled under the shade of the forest trees that surrounded the church. . . . Lieutenant Simmes [sic] was among them, for I was introduced to him and talked with him. I was introduced to a number of them by name and remembered them a long time, but cannot recall them now. There was an Indian among them and a tall elderly officer who was very talkative . . . . They were delighted with the flowers we took to them and crowded around to get them and have them pinned on their uniforms. The ladies of our party were not all who went to see them. Quite a number of others from the neighborhood were there, but none took flowers but us, tho' all contributed something for them to eat. . . . The elderly officer came up and remarked . . . that all should go into the church and have a prayer . . . . Then they all filed out, the visitors bringing up the

rear to watch the soldiers get into the various carts and drive off amid a multitude of earnest wishes for their welfare, and hopes they might safely get through the lines. . . . [The] next morning . . . we all rejoiced to learn that the party had crossed the Chowan river without meeting any of the enemy's gunboats. . . . I forgot to mention that the Confederates shook hands with all the lady visitors before they left.[26]

She was, of course, mistaken about the soldiers' attraction to the flowers, just as her father had erred in saying that the hungry men would only be interested in food. The memoirs of Col. Green, Captain Seckel and others make clear that an overriding interest of the men was, in fact, the ladies who brought the food and flowers, and their first exposure to feminine company after weeks in Yankee prisons.

Edmond McHorney of Coinjock, North Carolina, later recalled those days. He was a boy of seventeen at the time, and spent three days journeying by foot and boat across the region, smuggling food, and carrying messages. At one point Federal soldiers detained and questioned him extensively, but he deceived them and finally, pleading his youth, won release. He then continued, helping in any way he could in what had become a community effort to return the Rebel officers to their lines in safety.[27]

Richard B. Creecy, editor of Elizabeth City's *The Economist* wrote, in 1899, of attempting to persuade Captain Parker, who was then a circuit Judge, to write an account of his escape of *Maple Leaf*. He was not successful with Captain Parker, but he did not give up. Creecy mentioned Joseph Wilson, "one of our oldest and most esteemed citizens, who fed the Confederate captors of the Maple Leaf in the swamps of Currituck when they were pursued by Federal cavalry," Henrietta Walker, "whose husband . . . carried the captors across Currituck sound and took care of them in the Currituck swamps," and Ed McHarney, [sic] "who, when a boy of 17, with his brother and a companion, conveyed some of the Confederate captors in their boat to Yeopim Creek in Perquimans county, and thence piloted them across Chowan river into the Confederate lines."[28]

In later issues of the paper, Creecy continued his search for the story of the Maple Leaf, adding accounts that probably have some basis in truth, but have a distinct flavor of the yarns spun by old-timers sitting around the stove in a country store. Creecy admitted that since the story was first mentioned, "every old man has some bit of reminiscence of this brilliant achievement in the annals of the war." He was quick to point out, however, that it was *The Economist* that first set the story in "unsmiling type," saying the paper was "drawn to it as a feather in the Albemarle's cap of war."

One such tale relates that when the incident occurred, Captain Nathaniel Grandy, "high Sheriff," was spending much of his time in the swamps looking for a "buffalo bull" named Pete Burgess.[29] While scouring the swamps, Grandy "fell in with the Maple Leaf Confederate captors, and was introduced to Capt. Simms, [sic] who was commanding a squad of the captors. Capt. Simms taught Capt. Grandy . . . the back step drill. This was to deceive the enemy by walking backward into a swamp, so it looked like walking out of it. Grandy dodged Pete that way, when not pursuing him."

Another tells of Milt Snowden, who when a boy, hauled food to the Confederates who were dodging the Federal cavalry. Snowden "thinks now, as he thought then, that the Yankee cavalry did not really want to find the Confederate officers, because they would have had bloody work when they found them."[30]

Major Wheelan and his Union cavalry came close to capturing at least some of the Confederates, but in the end his efforts were without success. Luckily for the escapees, and thanks to the Northern newspapers, their general situation was well known in Richmond.

More specific information about the plight of the *Maple Leaf*'s survivors was provided on June 17, by Colonel Dougherty and Captain Seckel, the first of the escapees to reach Richmond. This information was passed to high levels of the Confederate government, coming to the attention Secretary of War James A. Seddon, the overworked former Federal as well as Confederate congressman, described by a visitor who called about this time as

Seddon

"a cadaverous but clever-looking man."[31] That same day, Seddon telegraphed Major General Daniel Harvey Hill, brother-in-law of the late "Stonewall" Jackson, and the same West Point graduate who had negotiated the protocol on exchanges and paroles, who was then at Petersburg:

> I am just informed by special messenger that the officers who lately took the steamer Maple Leaf in the bay and escaped from captivity are hid in Camden County, on the east side of the Pasquotank, near that river, being intercepted by cavalry force sent by General Dix to recapture them. This cavalry has pickets along the river, and at the bridge. A cavalry force threatening the bridge, if you could send it, or some boats crossed over, would enable them to escape. There was no difference of opinion as to their right to escape. The officers left were wounded.[32]

The Confederates tactics of hiding during the day and traveling at night with the help of local guides was eventually successful, causing the Union cavalry to abandon its efforts. On June 18, General Corcoran notified General Dix:

> A detailed report from Major Wheelan is just received. He was for six days actively and vigilantly employed in searching for the escaped prisoners, making severe marches and traversing three counties. He finally ascertained at Elizabeth City that they crossed in three detachments at the mouth of the Pasquotank River rounding the point of Pasquotank County into the Little River. Major Wheelan's action was prompt and vigorous, and he is much disappointed.[33]

Major Wheelan may have been disappointed, but it is highly probable that his cavalrymen were just as happy to abandon the strenuous and futile patrolling in and about the swamp, which would have been very warm work. Their quarry at least had the benefit of resting in the shade during the day.

According to Colonel Green, his party crossed the Pasquotank River near Elizabeth City, the Perquimans River near Belvidere,

and the Chowan River near Murfreesboro. Finally they reached the tracks of the Seaboard and Roanoke Railway near Boykins, Virginia.[34] This town in Southampton County, incidentally, was near the scene, thirty-two years earlier, of Nat Turner's bloody slave rebellion, which began a chain of events that helped propel the North and South to war.[35]

Green claimed that the Confederates were being chased by four regiments of Federal cavalry, which appears to have been an exaggeration. He may, however, have had some basis for that belief. Troop movements in the vicinity of Suffolk were vigorous. At the Battle of Brandy Station, on June 9, the Union Army had discovered the movement of General Robert E. Lee's Army of Northern Virginia. This was the beginning of the campaign that would eventually result in the Battle of Gettysburg. The Federal commander in Suffolk had been ordered to do all he could to occupy the Confederate Army.[36]

Notes

1. Wolf, "Capture of the Maple Leaf," p. 375. Although Currituck, Camden, and Pasquotank counties were within Union lines, to the extent that Federal outposts were scattered about, and Yankee patrols could go where they wished, local companies of Rebel home guards, or "guerrillas," were very active.

2. On July 7, 1863, Colonel Ludlow wrote to Army headquarters in Washington, stating, "After the escape, through the criminal negligence of the officer in charge, of the paroled Confederate Officers from the steamer Maple Leaf, I gave notice to [Colonel Robert] Ould [a former U.S. Attorney for the District of Columbia and Ludlow's Confederate counterpart as Agent of Exchange] that if ever recaptured, without exchange, they would be hung." Ludlow to Kelton, A.A.G., July 7, 1863, OR, Series 2, vol. 6, p. 89. Ould had written to Ludlow a week earlier, expressing the Confederate view. He claimed that after the prisoners arrived in Virginia, harsh treatment by Federal officials justified their breach of parole. "Up until that time they had little or no guard. Their imprisonment was nominal. When they reached Fortress Monroe [sic] you made it actual. You put them in places well deserving the name of dungeons, eighteen in a room fifteen feet square, with an armed sentinel always at the door." Ould to Ludlow, July 1, 1863, OR, Series 2, vol. 6, p. 70. Ould apparently thought, mistakenly, that the prisoners had been confined at Fort Monroe, rather than Fort Norfolk.

3. A photograph of General Corcoran maintaining a watchful eye over the ramparts of Fort Corcoran (located on the Potomac opposite Georgetown), is contained in the popular Time-Life Series, *The Civil War - First Blood*

59

(Alexandria, Va.: Time-Life Books, 1983), pp. 60-61. While a prisoner, Corcoran was one of the hostages selected by Brigadier General John H. Winder to be hung in the event the Federal government executed certain captured Rebel seamen whose service as privateers was being equated to piracy. Exchanged in August of 1862, Corcoran was invited to dine with President Lincoln, and soon promoted to Brigadier General. Roy P. Basler, ed., *The Collected Works of Abraham Lincoln* (New Brunswick, N.J.: Rutgers University Press, 1953) 5: 380-81.

4. The finding of the resulting court of inquiry was not unanimous, with two members holding "that the killing of Lt. Col. Kimball was unjustifiable, and that Brig Genl Corcoran is censurable for his hasty action therein." The third member found, with some equivocation, "that there can no criminality attach to the act and that no malicious intent is chargeable upon Brig. Genl. Corcoran - but that he was unjustifiable [*sic*] in discharging the fatal shot that deprived Lieut Col Kimball, 9th N.Y. Vols. of his life." Record of Proceedings of Court of Inquiry appointed by Major General John J. Peck, Headquarters, U.S. Forces, Suffolk, Virginia, May 6, 1863, to "examine into the circumstances attending the death of Lt. Col Edgar A. Kimball, 9th N.Y. Vols." NARA, Records of the Office of the Judge Advocate General, RG 153.

5. William Gladstone, "The Colonel's Messmate," *Civil War Times Illustrated*, September/October 1983, p. 74. A photograph of Lieutenant Colonel Kimball is included in the brief article.

6. An aggressive young man who progressed from private to captain to major in the course of thirteen months, Wheelan had already lost one brother in the war and would soon lose a second. He was sometimes referred to by his superiors as the "gallant little Major Wheelan." NARA, CSR of James M. Wheelan, 1st New York Mounted Rifles, RG 94.

7. *CMH*, vol. 5, *North Carolina*, by D. H. Hill, Jr., pp. 681-83. Reports of where the Rebels came ashore range from eight to forty-five—though a better estimate would be ten to fifteen—miles south of Cape Henry.

8. Wolf, "Capture of the Maple Leaf," 375. "Prison Life and Escape of Col. Green," 57.

9. Green, *My Life in Prison and Escape*, pp. 34-35. See also, Wolf, "Capture of the Maple Leaf," p. 375. "Prison Life and Escape of Col. Green," 58.

10. Morse, "Capture of the Maple Leaf," p. 307.

11. The veterans of the *Maple Leaf* spoke often of Dismal Swamp, which they welcomed for the concealment it offered.

12. Green, *My Life in Prison and Escape*, pp. 39-41. According to Green, when someone had a question, such as why they had changed direction or were

stopping, he would whisper it to the man ahead of him, who would relay it up the chain, and the answer would come back the same way.

13. Ibid., p. 43.

14. *CMH*, vol. 5, *North Carolina*, by D. H. Hill, Jr., pp. 681-83.

15. Yeary, *Reminiscences of the Boys in Gray*, p. 675.

16. Wolf, "Capture of the Maple Leaf," p. 375.

17. Haas, "Diary of Julius Giesecke," p. 32.

18. Green, *My Life in Prison and Escape*, 48.

19. "Prison Life and Escape of Col. Green," p. 59.

20. *Daily Richmond Examiner*, June 23, 1863.

21. Colonel Green describes Sanderlin as, "a good looking young man of about thirty years of age, unmistakably a gentleman as was easily to be seen . . . , a man of considerable culture, a lawyer by profession, had been a member of the state legislature, [who] knew the swamp and seemed possessed of all the knowledge of every character that could be of use to us in our situation." Green, *My Life in Prison and Escape*, p. 50.

22. Edna M. Shannonhouse, comp. and ed., *Yearbook - Pasquotank Historical Society* (Elizabeth City, N.C.: Pasquotank Historical Society, 1983), vol. 4, "The Two Wealthy Burgesses," by Edna M. Shannonhouse, p. 67, quoting from Jesse Pugh, *Two Hundred Years Along the Pasquotank - A Biographical History of Camden County* (Old Trap, NC: Jesse Pugh, 1967), p. 187. According to this account, another local citizen who risked "death, loss of property, and danger to his family" to assist the group is said to have been Samuel Leary, of Sandy Hook.

23. Wolf, "Capture of the Maple Leaf," p. 375. *Confederate Veteran* note re Edward D. Parker, 23 (January 1915): 41.

24. Haas, "Diary of Julius Giesecke," pp. 33-34.

25. Myers was commander of the Perquimans Partisan Rangers, later Company D of the 66th North Carolina Infantry. David A. Watson, *Perquimans County - A Brief History* (Raleigh: Division of Archives and History, Department of Cultural Resources, 1987), pp. 80-81.

26. Mrs. Christopher W. Hollowell, "The Maple Leaf," *Elizabeth City Economist*, September 1, 1899. The Indian may have been Lieutenant J. M. Mobley, of the 1st Choctaw Battalion. The elderly officer was most likely either the sixty-year-old Captain Leclerc Fusilier, or fifty-year-old Edward McGowan. Both had reputations as great story-tellers.

27. Reminiscences of Edmond McHorney, manuscript in possession of his great-grandson, J. Rives Manning, of Roanoke Rapids, N.C. *Elizabeth City Economist*, September 8, 1899. McHorney was probably the young guide spoken of by Green and others.

28. *Elizabeth City Economist*, August 18, 1899. Richard Benbury Creecy, *Grandfather's Tales of North Carolina History* (Raleigh: Edwards & Broughton, Printers, 1901), pp. 264-67. *Elizabeth City Economist*, September 8, 1899.

29. "Buffalo" was a term applied locally to Northern sympathizers.

30. *Elizabeth City Economist*, September 8, 1899.

31. Arthur James Fremantle, *The Fremantle Diary*, ed. Walter Lord (Boston: Little, Brown and Company, 1954), p. 170.

32. Seddon to Hill, June 17, 1863, *OR*, Series 1, vol. 27, pt. 3, p. 901.

33. Corcoran to Dix, June 18, 1863, *OR*, Series 1, vol. 27, pt. 3, p. 206. Major Wheelan had been similarly frustrated just a few days earlier. Union General John J. Peck wrote General Dix on June 8, "It gives me pleasure to advise you that Major [James N.] Wheelan made a movement before daylight upon a guerrilla party near South Mills. . . . The party would have been secured had not his approach been signaled by a woman." Peck to Dix, June 8, 1863, *OR*, Series 1, vol. 27, pt. 2, p. 786.

34. Browne, "Stranger than Fiction," pp. 181-85.

35. See Stephen B. Oates, *The Fires of Jubilee: Nat Turner's Fierce Rebellion* (New York: Harper & Row, 1975).

36. Halleck to Dix, June 14, 1863, *OR*, series 1, vol. 27, pt. 3, p. 111.

Chapter 5

We Had a Good Time

General Hill's Rebel cavalry located some of the men from the *Maple Leaf*, screening them from any threat of recapture.[1] However, even those without the protection of an escort made their way to safety, all seventy eventually reaching the junction of Weldon, North Carolina, by way of the Seaboard and Roanoke Railway. (See map at page 47.) The Petersburg and Weldon Railway then took them some sixty miles to Petersburg, where they began the final leg of their journey to Richmond, only another twenty-five miles further north.

On June 22, the noisy locomotive of the Richmond & Petersburg line chugged into the Confederate capital, pulling a train carrying sixty-three of the men from the *Maple Leaf*, as well as Captain Sanderlin, who insisted on escorting the men the entire way.[2] The possibility of their arrival had been signaled four days earlier by Dougherty and Seckel,[3] who brought the information on their location to Secretary Seddon. Welcoming the Rebel officers was an occasion for celebration and warm greetings, the more so since good news was scarce in the city that week.[4] According to Morse, "We entered the Confederate capital a dirty, fagged out, used up, but as happy a set of 'rebs' as ever wore the gray; and the wondering spectators on the crowded thoroughfares might have readily mistaken us for wild men of the forest, for such our unkempt locks, sun-browned visage and tattered covering bespoke us."

Many of the fugitives from the *Maple Leaf* enjoyed a welcome rest at the Spotswood Hotel, the most luxurious in the city. Opened only in 1860, it played a prominent role in Richmond society. Its guests had included most of the Southern leadership, and it was the choice temporary residence of Jefferson Davis when the Confederate Capital moved from Montgomery to Richmond.[5]

The provost marshal and local military commander in Richmond was Brigadier General John H. Winder, age sixty-three and a veteran of the Mexican War. He was a member of the U.S.

THE CONFEDERATE STATES OF AMERICA, Dr.

CONDITIONS AND EXPLANATION.	When.	For.	Rate per Month.		Amount per Month.		ARREARS.
			Months	Days	Dollars	Cents	Dollars	Cents
For pay as	183	1865						
	21 July	31 May	3" "		195	—	585	00
For								
Forage for								
							$585	00

I hereby certify that the foregoing account is correct and just; that I have not been absent, without leave, during any part of the time charged; that I have not received pay, forage, or received anything in lieu of any part thereof, for any part of the time therein charged; that the horses were actually kept in service and were mustered for the whole of the time charged; that for the whole of the time charged for my self appointment I actually and legally held the appointment and did duty in the department; that I have been commissioned duties to the number of years stated in the charge for every additional five years' service; that I am not in arrears with the Confederate States on any account whatsoever; and that the last payment I received was from _____, and to the 28 day of _____.

Let the sum above acknowledge that I have received of _____ the 28 day of _____ being the amount in full of _____ account.

Pay, ... $
Forage, " ....

Amount, $ 585.00

(Signed Duplicates)

Military Academy's class of 1820 and later served there as professor of tactics. Winder received the entire group of seventy men after they had a night's rest and an opportunity make themselves presentable. After asking them to relate how they had escaped, and what they had been through, Winder called for the paymaster who settled all claims for wages due.[6]

Many of the Confederates had a fair sum coming to them. On June 23, Colonel Witt collected $585, representing three months pay. In a moment of exuberance, he scrawled across the bottom of his pay voucher, "I escaped the Maple Leaf."[7]

While the money was welcome, the Rebels were probably disappointed at the loss in value of the Confederate dollar. Green relates, "I purchased a new cavalry jacket, made of gray cassinett, for one hundred and twenty-five dollars in Richmond. That and my hotel bill and traveling expenses home [to Tennessee] consumed about five months pay or one thousand dollars." Between 1861 and 1863, flour had risen from $7 to $28 a barrel, bacon from 20 cents to $2.25 a pound, dinner at a first class hotel to $25 a sitting, and postage for a letter home to 50 cents.[8]

Inflation notwithstanding, the Confederate capital was a busy and exciting city, and ample entertainment was available for those whose pockets were full. Captain Giesecke noted in his diary that on the day after he reached the city, he stayed in bed all day; the next two days he noted only that "we had a good time."[9]

Captain Semmes found that his mother was visiting the city, having recently been expelled from the North, and they enjoyed a brief but happy reunion. Colonel Witt took advantage of his visit to the capital by contacting officials in the Confederate War Department regarding his uncertain future, his regiment being among those still under siege at Port Hudson.[10] On June 26, Lieutenant Robert Noland wrote his sister from Richmond, describing his adventures. A member of the Fort Norfolk Group, he may have worried about the argument just before leaving the *Maple Leaf* over the legality of the escape, and whether it was a violation of his parole; or, he may have believed—as he told his sister—that having a hand in the capture of the *Maple Leaf* made him a pirate; in any case he advised her, "destroy this letter."[11]

In taking their farewells before leaving Richmond, the Rebel officers expressed their gratitude to Captain Sanderlin, who would not accept money, by presenting him with a new Colt revolver, the only one they could find in the city.[12] They then set out, travelling alone or in small groups, to rejoin their various commands and comrades in the field.

Although Green and his companions had made a fairly quick (three day) trip from St. Louis to Fort Norfolk, and the travel of the escaped Confederates from Weldon to Richmond was reasonably rapid, travel in the South was not always as easy. The effort of Captain Giesecke to rejoin his company was probably typical of the experience of many of the soldiers returning to their regiments.

Along with several companions, Giesecke departed Richmond on June 27, traveling by train through Wilmington, North Carolina, and the South Carolina railroad junctions of Kingsville and Branchville. From there, other trains took them through the Georgia cities of Augusta and Atlanta. In Alabama, they passed through Montgomery, Selma, and Demopolis. Next came the Mississippi towns of Meridian, Jackson, Brookhaven and Natchez. Finally, in Louisiana, their voyage took them to Trinity, Holloways Prairie, Alexandria, Washington, Opelousas, and, at last, New Iberia.

Travel was often interrupted. At Montgomery, a visit to the local Provost Marshal caused Giesecke to lose a day's travel when he missed the boat down the Alabama River to Selma. At Natchez, he was obliged to wait for the departure of Union gunboats before crossing the Mississippi, and at Alexandria, Louisiana (where, on July 13, he received news of the fall of Vicksburg), he could get space on the "stage" to Washington, Louisiana, only after waiting five days, and then traveling as a "deck passenger." While they would sometimes pass the night at hotels, on several occasions, particularly when on foot, Giesecke and his companions would stay with whoever along the road might be willing to have them, which however, does not seem to have been a problem.

In any event, on July 20, twenty-four days after leaving Richmond, Giesecke rejoined his regiment at New Iberia. It was the end of a journey that involved eleven railways, two boats, three stage coaches, two hired carriages, and four days of walking.[13]

Notes

1. Wolf, "Capture of the Maple Leaf," p. 375.

2. Five of the men, Pruett, Andrews, Carmouche, Gilbau and Jeter, arrived in Richmond earlier the same day, and took rooms at the Linwood House. *Daily Richmond Examiner*, June 23, 1863.

3. *The Richmond Enquirer*, June 23, 1863. See also Tyler and Allegre, column dated June 24, 1863, in the paper's June 26, 1863, edition. Dougherty and Seckel, apparently set off on their own for Richmond after crossing the Pasquotank, and arrived there on June 17th.

4. Newspapers carried stories of the sieges at Vicksburg and Port Hudson as well as the great cavalry engagement at Brandy Station.

5. A. A. Hoehling and Mary Hoehling, *the Last Days of the Confederacy* (New York: The Fairfax Press, 1981), p. 5-6.

6. *SHSP.*, "Thrilling Incident," p. 165.

7. NARA, CSR of Allen Rufus Witt, 10th Arkansas Infantry, RG 109.

8. Green, *My Life in Prison and Escape*, p. 51. Shelby Foote, *The Civil War - A Narrative*, vol 2, *Fredericksburg to Meridian* (New York: Random House, 1963), pp. 159-160. Bell Irvin Wiley, *The Life of Johnny Reb - The Common Soldier of the Confederacy* (Baton Rouge: Louisiana State University Press, 1943), p. 196.

9. Haas, "Diary of Julius Giesecke," 34.

10. W. Adolph Roberts, *Semmes of the Alabama* (New York: The Bobbs-Merrill Company, 1938), 223. NARA, Witt to Seddon, June 27, 1863, Letters Received by the Confederate Secretary of War. RG 109.

11. Unattributed note pertaining to Lieutenant Robert Noland, *Confederate Veteran* 20 (June 1912): 272.

12. Green, *My Life in Prison and Escape*, p. 50.

13. Haas, "Diary of Julius Giesecke," pp. 34-36. For an account of travel along virtually the same route as Giesecke's journey—though the month before and going in the opposite direction—see *Fremantle Diary*, pp. 60-117, 137-75.

Chapter 6

Scour the Country in Every Direction

As soon as he returned to Fort Monroe and learned of the escape, General Dix ordered Colonel Ludlow to find how it happened. Ludlow questioned the ship's officers and a few of the prisoners, and concluded that the escape was caused by Lieutenant Dorsey's failure to properly perform his duties as commander of the guard. Specifically, Ludlow found that the guards had not loaded their muskets, that Dorsey had not ordered the Sergeant of the Guard to have them loaded, and that, since he had not inspected the guard, Dorsey did not know whether they were loaded or not. In addition, Ludlow reported that, in his opinion, if Lieutenant Dorsey had performed his duties correctly, some of the prisoners (presumably meaning those of the Fort Norfolk group who had given their "parole") would have helped him maintain order.[1] (See Ludlow's report at Appendix C.)

The success of the escape was mainly due to the help provided by the residents of North Carolina communities near Currituck Sound, Camden Court House, Elizabeth City, and elsewhere along the Rebels' route. This assistance was apparent to Union commanders, and there are fragmentary stories of the Federal army arresting citizens and destroying boats in connection with the episode. Less than two months later a Federal officer recommended the destruction of all boats in the vicinity of Elizabeth City, claiming that he had destroyed them all the previous May, but that some had reappeared.[2]

During the following months, Federal expeditions into Camden, Currituck, and Pasquotank Counties attempted to engage and destroy the Rebel militia, and generally punished those not loyal to the Union. By December some residents were in much the same predicament as many civilians in the Republic of Vietnam a hundred years later. That is, whether they wanted to or not, they were expected to help the guerrilla forces, many of whom were their friends, neighbors, and relatives, by supplying them with food, clothing, and other assistance. On the other hand, the Union

Army strictly prohibited aid or comfort to the guerrillas, and severely punished those who disobeyed. The orders Brigadier General Henry M. Naglee issued to the 5th Pennsylvania Cavalry, in September 1863, were typical:

> Scour the country in every direction and get rid of the few guerrillas that remain in Camden and Currituck Counties . . . . Allow no person to pass out whatever . . . . Send me daily reports and communicate all the names of suspicious persons . . . . Advise Mrs. Bell that after ten days her house will be destroyed unless she removes the guerrilla Sanderlin from it. Advise others to the same purpose who permit their houses to be occupied by guerrillas or their families. Report all persons that give aid and comfort to guerrillas. A severe policy must be adopted in regard to them.[3]

Aided by a variety of informers and Union supporters, Federal commanders sought out rebel sympathizers. Many of those who had helped the Rebels escape would pay with lost wagons and livestock, or worse yet, burned homes.

The largest of the expeditions was that led by Brigadier General Edward A. Wild in December 1863. Wild's force consisted of the 2d North Carolina Colored Volunteers and the 1st and 5th U.S. Colored Troops, augmented by cavalry and artillery—in all just short of two thousand men. Although the expedition captured only a few Rebels (one of whom was summarily executed after a perfunctory "court-martial" convicted him of being a member of a guerrilla force), by his own estimate Wild burned over two-dozen homesteads. In addition, he confiscated property filling several hundred wagons (also confiscated) and the livestock necessary to pull them. What was viewed as a greater outrage was his taking four people hostage, three women and an old man. The expedition's most significant accomplishment was the liberation of some 2,500 slaves, however Wild (who was seeking recruits for his "African Brigade," as it was then designated) complained that, "few results were gained, as the able bodied negroes have had ample opportunities for escape heretofore . . . ."[4]

Wild's raid was characterized by excessive harshness and wholesale confiscation of personal property, with many pro-Union families later complaining that they were treated no better than their Rebel-sympathizing neighbors. Substantiated claims and complaints caused General Butler to dismiss some of the officers (all white) responsible, and to threaten severe measures in the event of further such excesses.

One story tells of the Federal Army's arrest of Nancy White, a ten-year-old girl whose family lived on Knotts Island, because of her father's aid to the Rebels escaping the *Maple Leaf*.[5] Although Nancy's father, William Henry White, had assisted the escaping Rebels, it appears that Nancy was taken hostage (and her home burned) on December 21, 1863, because General Wild believed her father to be a lieutenant in the local Rebel guerrilla company of Captain John T. Coffee. It is likely, nevertheless, that the Yankees also knew about his assistance to the Rebels from the *Maple Leaf* six months earlier. In any case, Nancy spent several weeks confined at Norfolk before being released January, 1864.[6]

Notes

1. NARA, Ludlow to Dix, June 12, 1863, RG 94, (Appendix C). This is probably what those who remained with the *Maple Leaf* told Ludlow.

2. Report of Captain W. Dewees Roberts, Commanding 11th Pennsylvania Cavalry at South Mills, N.C., August 12, 1863, *OR*, Series 1, vol. 29, pt. 1, p. 31.

3. Naglee to Lewis, September 12, 1864, *OR*, Series 1, vol. 29, pt. 2, p. 174.

4. J. V. Witt, *Every Species of Property*, unpublished manuscript in possession of the author. General Wild's report on the expedition is found in Wild to Johnston, December 28, 1863, *OR*, Series 1, vol. 29, pt. 1, pp. 910-18.

5. Browne, "Stranger than Fiction," p. 184. R. H. Worthington, "The Maple Leaf," *Norfolk Ledger-Dispatch*, October 3, 1935. Manuscript account of Alyda White Beasley, great-granddaughter of William Henry White [Sr.]. Special Collections, Currituck County Library, Currituck, N.C.

6. Based on an interview with Dale Beasley, great-great-nephew of Nancy White Dey, Knotts Island, Currituck County, North Carolina, July 17, 1992. It appears that Nancy's age was closer to twenty than ten when she was taken away.

Chapter 7

Where Are Those Gallant Fellows?

With Colonel Ludlow's investigation complete and the Confederate officers back within their lines, the episode of the *Maple Leaf* was soon forgotten—eclipsed by other adventures, hardships and tragedies. A brief recital of what later became of them, as well as the places they had been and the ships involved, completes the tale.

The Yankees

By late 1863, exchanges were at a low point. The Federal Army was holding the majority of prisoners, but was reluctant to allow their exchange because it would replenish the diminishing manpower of the South.[1] Already complicated, the system was further frustrated by the North's insistence, and the South's refusal, to exchange white and black soldiers on an equal basis. Exchanges occurred, but these were exceptions, rather than routine practice. Adding to the deterioration of the system, the War Department replaced Colonel Ludlow with an officer less familiar with the arrangements for exchanges and paroles, by now highly complex. Ludlow · was assigned to other staff duties for the remainder of the war, and was later promoted to brevet brigadier general, U.S. Volunteers.

Major Wheelan, whose cavalry had unsuccessfully pursued the Confederates in and around Dismal Swamp, reached the grade of Lieutenant Colonel by the end of the war, and in 1867 was promoted to brevet colonel for gallantry and meritorious service.[2]

Ill feelings over General Corcoran's killing of Colonel Kimball persisted. On August 17, 1863, Corcoran wrote to President Lincoln (who he had met with a week earlier, and who he had dined with at the White House after his release from prison in 1862), asking to be reassigned.[3] Then, four months later, Corcoran was killed accidentally when he was thrown or fell from his horse while riding with several member of his staff near Fairfax Court House, Virginia.[4]

In July of 1863, the Army transferred General Dix from Fort Monroe to New York, replacing him with General John Foster, and four months later, General Benjamin Butler. Thereafter, Dix held only staff positions until the end of the war. Later, he became a diplomat and was elected Governor of New York. Fort Dix, New Jersey, which until recently was one of the Army's largest basic training centers, was named in his honor.

After the South's surrender, Major General Butler served five terms as a member of the U.S. House of Representatives. A Radical Republican, he was a leader of the nearly successful effort to remove Andrew Johnson from the Presidency. He also served a term as governor of Massachusetts.

As mentioned earlier, in April of 1864, at Mansfield (Sabine Cross Roads), General Banks once again confronted General Richard Taylor, who earlier had eluded his trap at Irish Bend. After the Confederate success at Mansfield, which ended his Red River campaign, Banks withdrew his Army and was never again given field command. After the war he served as a several terms in the House of Representatives.

On June 12, 1863, Colonel William Wilson's 6th New York Infantry marched off the *Cahawba* and down Broadway, along with "Billy" their whiskey-drinking mascot, who "marched proudly at the head of the column with his horns decked with ribbons." At City Hall Park Barracks they stacked their arms—they thought for the last time. Just a few days later, however, when the New York draft riots broke out, citizens of Staten Island petitioned Governor Seymour to have Wilson reform as much of his regiment as possible to help maintain order. "The hard brown faces of the veterans of the Sixth at that time were enough to frighten the very souls out of an ordinary mob. . . . This creditable piece of duty was the last one performed by Col. Wilson and the men of his regiment."[5] Wilson later sought command of the 69th New York Infantry, but Washington did not want any more to do with him. His records include a May 2, 1864, order directing General George Meade to take measures to prevent Wilson from being mustered in to Federal service without special permission. Unaccountably, those same records also contain an order, dated three years later (June 22, 1867), appointing Wilson to the grade

of brevet brigadier general, "for gallantry and meritorious service during the war."[6]

Lieutenant Dorsey, who had commanded the guard detail on the *Maple Leaf*, left the U.S. Army in disgrace. Administratively dismissed by direction of the president on June 20, 1863, eight days after General Dix received Lieutenant Colonel Ludlow's report of investigation (see Appendix C), he was denied the benefit of a court-martial where he might have established that he was not solely responsible for the escape.[7]

The Rebel Prisoners

Captain Semmes, the elected leader of the Confederates after they reached shore, was later promoted to major and served actively and with distinction until the end of the war. As General Taylor's Chief of Artillery, he took part in the April 1864 defeat of General Banks at Mansfield, possibly unaware that one of his West Point classmates, Union Captain James A. Sanderson, was mortally wounded in that action. After the war, Semmes was a well-known lawyer, judge, and member of the Alabama legislature, making substantial contributions to the revision of the civil code of Alabama.[8]

After his twenty-four day journey from Richmond to New Iberia, Louisiana, Captain Giesecke rejoined his unit, and also fought with General Taylor's army at Mansfield and Pleasant Hill. After the war he returned to Texas, raised a family, and eventually became one of the owners of the German language New Braunfels newspaper, *Neu-Braunfelser Zeitung*, which in 1934 and 1935 published his Civil War diary.[9]

Captain Fusilier, the elderly but hard-fighting Louisiana planter, also rejoined General Richard Taylor's command and was taken prisoner a second time. But he got away again. According to Taylor, "Fusilier escaped while descending the Teche on a steamer by springing from the deck to seize the overhanging branch of a live oak. The guard fired on him, but darkness and the rapid movement of the steamer were in his favor, and he got off unhurt."[10]

Captain Seckel, the young man enraptured by Adelaide Campbell during the long trek through Dismal Swamp, returned to the staff of M. Jeff Thompson. As a part of that command, he joined in General Sterling Price's last raid into Missouri. He was retired and was living in Paris, Texas, at the time he wrote his reminiscences.[11]

Colonel Allen Rufus Witt, returned to Arkansas where he reformed his regiment, which became known as the 10th Arkansas Cavalry, and which also participated in Price's 1864 raid. Although the 3d Arkansas (U.S.) Cavalry forced Witt's regiment to disperse in the spring of 1865, he continued to act as commander of the 10th Arkansas, and negotiated for most of his men to swear allegiance to the Union at Jacksonport, Arkansas, in June of 1865. After the war he served in the Arkansas Senate until the 1866-67 legislature was dissolved as a result of the 1867 Congressional Reconstruction Act. State authorities later appointed him brigadier general of militia.[12]

Colonel Green returned to duty, serving under the command of Major General Nathan Bedford Forrest. After the war Green prospered as owner of a large farm near Covington, Kentucky. In 1887 he moved to Covington proper, where he did editorial work on the *Tipton County Record*. He continued writing stories of his experiences in the Civil War, which this author has quoted so often, until his death in 1906.[13]

After the war, McGowan spent some time in New York, served briefly as Assistant Sergeant at Arms of the U.S. House of Representatives, and eventually returned to San Francisco, where he died in 1893. Views as to his character are wide-ranging but never weakly stated, some claiming he was "unprincipled," and a "friend of criminals and ward heelers . . . an example of the worst sort of magistrate."[14] At the other end of the spectrum, are those who praised him as the most gifted man to be drawn to the California by the gold rush of 1849. Author John Myers Myers predicted that future generations of honest historians would find McGowan's writings "the largest body of reliable source material bearing on the era," and similarly, that literary experts would award McGowan "the priority as a poet and a wit that has been his neglected due for over a century."[15]

The twenty-seven men who chose to remain in Federal custody on the *Maple Leaf*, were held only briefly at Fort Delaware. As a

77

NARRATIVE

OF

EDWARD McGOWAN,

INCLUDING A FULL ACCOUNT OF THE

Your friend,
Edw McGowan

Author's Adventures and Perils, while persecuted by the
San Francisco Vigilance Committee of 1856.

PUBLISHED BY THE AUTHOR.

1857.

result of overcrowding and illness, on July 15, 1863, the Commissary General of Prisoners directed that all officers be transferred to Johnson's Island, located a mile from shore in Lake Erie, near Sandusky, Ohio.[16] The prison at Johnson's Island consisted of wooden barracks constructed specifically for the purpose of housing approximately 1,000 prisoners of war.[17] A roll of prisoners there includes the names of fifteen officers who remained with the *Maple Leaf* when others escaped; three of them died within six months, possibly of wounds inflicted before their capture, although the roll indicates that their deaths were due to disease.[18]

Captain Fuller, the former captain of the *Cotton*, and later of the *Queen of the West*, and the leader of the Rebels on the *Maple Leaf*, was one of those who died at Johnson's Island, having succumbed on July 25, only a few weeks after the escape.[19] His reputation as a fighter was such that, even three months after his death, rumors born of hope spread among worried and anxious soldiers, that Fuller was again with the Confederate Navy at Sabine Pass.[20] In General Taylor's view, "a braver man never lived."[21]

Another officer whose illness prevented his escape from the *Maple Leaf* was Captain Asbury, who was sick in the hold of the ship when it was captured. Taken to Fort Delaware, and then to Johnson's Island, Asbury was released on parole the following March, and sent to Demopolis, Alabama to await exchange a month later. Before returning to his command in the Trans-Mississippi, Asbury accepted an invitation to spend a week at a plantation near Eutaw, Alabama, the home of two sisters named Ridgeway. The contrast to prison life was described by Asbury:

> The ladies entertained us delightfully; we spent the
> hours like minutes and the week like a day; we
> fished, hunted and rode; the negroes danced for us
> and sung their Southern songs; the ladies played
> beautifully on the piano; we made love to them and
> sung our war songs and told war stories. But the
> parting time came, and with leaden hearts and long,
> regretful farewells, we separated forever.[22]

Finding that his old regiment had been destroyed, Asbury reported to his new commander, General Shelby, at Jacksonport, Arkansas. Later, during Sterling Price's 1864 raid into Missouri, he fell in with "Bloody Bill" Anderson, who led a faction of the former Quantrill Gang. Asbury was present when Anderson was killed near Richmond, Missouri, on October 26, 1864.[23] He continued briefly with the guerrilla band, now led by Archie Clements, whom he considered a friend. Then, Asbury states, "when we reached the county from which I had started into the war—Texas—being well acquainted with the people and the roads, and not approving of some of the acts of the command I was with, I concluded to leave it and work out my own salvation."[24]

In the years after the war, Asbury became president of the American Bank in Higgensville, Missouri, and wrote of the events on the *Maple Leaf*, as "one of the most daring acts of the war," stating "those were stirring times. We did not have chicken pie and ice cream every day for dinner."[25] Although Asbury was guilty of understandable hyperbole, the safe return of the liberated prisoners brought a welcome breeze of good news, however brief, to Richmond.

The Other Rebels

Secretary of War Seddon, who had urged General Hill to assist the survivors of the *Maple Leaf*, resigned in February of 1865. He then returned to his home, Sabot Hill, where, despite his unhealthy appearance, he lived another fifteen years, attaining the advanced age of eighty. General D. H. Hill, who had negotiated the protocol on exchanges and paroles, and whose cavalry was sent to assist the fugitives, also survived the war. He then entered the newspaper business and later became president of the predecessor to the University of Arkansas.

Captain Sanderlin and his men continued to trouble the Yankees throughout the remaining months of the war, surviving numerous attempts aimed their eradication. By 1865, Sanderlin was a major in the state militia. After Appomattox, he became a merchant in Shiloh, North Carolina. He also operated a plantation known as the Bear Garden. He later disposed of his various properties in that area and moved to Virginia.

Seven years after she and her friends brought flowers to the Rebel officers at Bethel Church, Parthenia Gatling married one of the most prominent citizens of the county, Christopher W. Hollowell, forty-eight years old and a widower. During the war Hollowell was considered a reliable Union man by Federal commanders, but at the same time he has been described by Southern sympathizers as the "good samaritan" of the local community during the war.[26]

After the Confederate surrender, Federal authorities detained Colonel Robert Ould, Confederate Agent of Exchange, on charges that he had misappropriated property belonging to Federal soldiers taken prisoner. Several weeks later, they dismissed the charges and released Ould, who later resumed the practice of law, but in Richmond rather than Washington.

Richard Taylor ended the war as a lieutenant general. Afterward, he worked at restoring the communities of southern Louisiana, and wrote a history of the war that, in the opinion of one distinguished Civil War scholar, demonstrated that he "possessed literary art that approached first rank."[27]

In November 1864, seventeen months after General Winder had welcomed the veterans of the *Maple Leaf* to Richmond, the Confederate Government placed him in charge of all prisoners of the Confederacy east of the Mississippi. However, three months later he died, some say due to overwork at "a task made impossible by the inadequacy of supplies of men, food, clothing and Medicines." Others claim that had he lived, the Federal Army would have tried and hanged him, rather than Major Henry Wirz, Commandant of the Confederate prisoner of war camp at Andersonville, Georgia, for mistreatment of Federal soldiers in Confederate prisons. Mary Chesnut, in her diary entry for February 10, 1865, wrote "Yesterday [Major] General [Mansfield] Lovell dined here and then they went to poor old Winder's funeral. Well, Winder is safe from the wrath to come. General Lovell suggested that if the Yankees ever caught Winder, 'it would go hard with him.'"[28]

By coincidence, General Corcoran when writing earlier of his days as a prisoner of the Confederates, had spoken kindly of Winder. Telling of a news report in one of the Northern papers describing how Winder supposedly had ordered him placed in irons for refusing to answer when the roll was called, Corcoran stated:

> Not only was this entirely untrue, but there never was the slightest foundation for it. General Winder always did all in his power, as far as consistent with existing rules and orders, to make the prisoners under his charge as comfortable as possible.[29]

The Places

Gratiot Street Military Prison. After the war, the Gratiot Street Military Prison in St. Louis was no longer needed. Damaged during several escape attempts and fires, the building was allowed to fall into further disrepair, and eventually was destroyed. No signs of its existence remain at its former site on the northwest corner of 8th and Gratiot.

Fort Norfolk. Described as one of the best preserved examples of seventeenth century seacoast fortification, and the only surviving example of the type constructed with a semicircular face, Fort Norfolk has endured quite well. In 1923 it became headquarters to the Norfolk District, U.S. Army Corps of Engineers, which continues to use the structure, portions of which are being restored. Workers there recently discovered graffiti—previously hidden by paneling—scratched into the walls by prisoners. Some of the graffiti, now preserved, expresses common complaints concerning food and the confiscation of the prisoners' personal property. There is also the name, "E. S. Parker," which may have been carved by Captain Edward S. Parker, the young lawyer from Goldsboro, who had become Quartermaster of the 50th North Carolina.[30]

The U.S. Customhouse, New Orleans. This large and ornate building was finally completed at a cost of $5 million. During Reconstruction, it played a role in the 1874 "Battle of Liberty Place," as the left anchor of General Longstreet's line defending against the White League.[31] The building continues in full use today, host to various Federal activities, predominantly those of the U.S. Customs Service, occupying a full block at 423 Canal Street.[32]

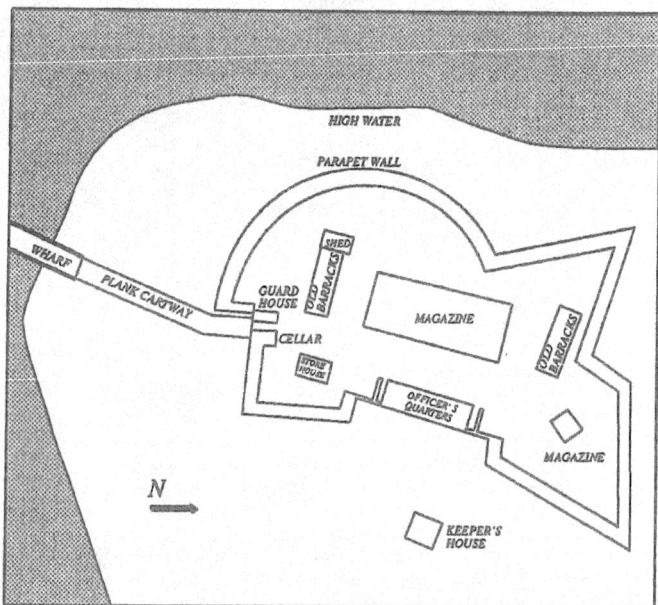

FORT NORFOLK

(Not to Scale)

Grafitti left by prisoners was recently found on the
walls in the building marked "OFFICER'S QUARTERS".
The author believes, however, that the complaints
of Col. Green and others had to do with conditions in the
building marked "MAGAZINE" which has a single
window in the wall facing the water.

Fort Monroe. At the close of the Civil War, Jefferson Davis was imprisoned here until his release in 1867. The Army has continuously occupied Fort Monroe, and has constructed numerous buildings outside the walls of the old fort, which remains essentially intact. Today Fort Monroe is Headquarters of the U.S. Army Training and Doctrine Command, charged with—among other things—supervision of the Army's schools and training centers. The Casemate Museum, located within the old fort, preserves the cell in which Jefferson Davis was confined. The museum's Civil War and coast artillery collections attract thousands of visitors yearly.[33]

The Spotswood Hotel. This Richmond landmark, located on the southeast corner of 8th and Main, survived the fires that destroyed much of the city at the end of the war, and served as the residence of news reporters and other visitors after Appomattox. It lasted only a few years, however, and was finally destroyed by fire on Christmas Eve, 1870.[34]

Fort Delaware. Before the war ended some 2,700 prisoners died at Fort Delaware, "more because of the unhealthy conditions on the island and the backwardness of the medical science of that day than from intentional neglect," and are buried at Finn's Point, New Jersey. If the climate was unhealthy, at least the food was above average, the prison bakery being highly praised by many veterans. A principal cause of illness was the water, and one veteran is quoted as saying that, "the water was full of 'wiggle waggles' and large ones being the product of the Jersey mosquito but they were harmless when killed by a mixture of whiskey or brandy which we were allowed to get from the sutler." Fort Delaware is now a state park open for tours during summer months.[35]

Johnson's Island. Although very little remains to identify Johnson's Island as host to a prison camp, like Civil War sites scattered throughout the country, it has become the subject of contest between preservationists and developers. Several lawsuits have been filed over the future of the site, and whether it will be preserved or altered to make room for a private marina.[36]

Today, in the North Carolina counties of Camden, Currituck, and Pasquotank there are several prosperous but sparsely populated

VIEW OF JOHNSON'S ISLAND,

SANDUSKY BAY.

THE ARRIVAL OF TWO THOUSAND VICKSBURG PRISONERS AT FORT DELAWARE.—[SKETCHED BY MR. H. ALES, PENNSYLVANIA VOLS.]

villages. The largest community, Elizabeth City, was founded two hundred years ago. With many fine old homes and a thirty-block historic district, it attracts thousands of tourists each year, many on their way to or from the vacation favorites, Nags Head and the Cape Hatteras National Seashore.

The Ships

The *Cahawba*. The Army purchased the *Cahawba* on May 1, 1864 for $135,000. When the war ended eleven months later, she was sold for $16,500, or twelve percent of the purchase price. Even considering wartime inflation and demand for vessels, it would appear that the Army either paid too much or received too little for the vessel. One suspects the former, since in 1867 the ship was scrapped.[37]

The *Utica*. After the war, the already elderly *Utica* was returned to her commercial owners and continued in service until 1875, and finally abandoned in 1888, by which time she would have been in service for fifty-two years. Since this is unlikely, some have concluded that the owners probably neglected to have her name removed from the rolls of active vessels until long after she no longer existed."[38]

The *Maple Leaf*. Eight months after the incident recounted here, the *Maple Leaf* was sent to Florida, where it served at times as the flagship of General Truman Seymore. During the early morning hours of April 1, 1864, the *Maple Leaf* descended the St. Johns River toward Jacksonville, returning from a voyage to Palatka. Some sixty persons were on board, including, in addition to the ship's officers and crew, three ladies, at least one of whom was the wife of a Federal officer, "Mrs. Captain [Peter Remsen] Chadwick." The ship was carrying the camp and garrison equipment of three regiments of General Foster's brigade, the 13th Indiana, and the 112th and 169th New York, as well as the officers' personal baggage. In addition, she carried the stock of two sutlers, valued at $20,000.

At about 4:00 A.M. the ship struck a mine which exploded with such force as to "throw the bow of the steamer completely out of the water." Four men sleeping on deck near the forecastle, two firemen and two deck hands, were killed in the explosion. The remainder of those on the *Maple Leaf* boarded the ship's small

90

boats, and within a few hours made the trip down river to Jacksonville, a distance of approximately twelve miles. "Apprehensions that the Rebels on shore might put out and capture the entire party prevented them . . . from attempting to save anything but their own persons," and nothing "to the value of sixpence was saved."[39]

The *Maple Leaf*, protected by the heavy mud of the St. Johns, has rested in the river ever since. It has been described as, "the most important repository of Civil War artifacts ever found," and unsurpassed as a source for Civil War material culture." Since 1984, ship has been the primary concern of St. Johns Archaeological Expeditions, Inc., founded by Jacksonville dentist, Keith Holland, which seeks to collect all information regarding the *Maple Leaf*, as well as the retrieval of artifacts and their conservation, interpretation and display. Dr. Holland's group is allied with, and supported by, the State of Florida, the U.S. Army, and the Jacksonville Historical Society. Support is also provided by East Carolina University, which uses the project as an underwater classroom, and the Jacksonville Museum of Science and History, which has a permanent exhibit on the *Maple Leaf*. The recovery of artifacts resumed in the summer of 1993.[40]

It is not surprising that the seizure of the *Maple Leaf* has been given little attention considering its relative unimportance in comparison with preceding and subsequent events, the escape of seventy Rebel officers being but a minor footnote to a calamitous war filled with disasters. The day before the escape from the *Maple Leaf*, the largest cavalry battle of the war was fought at Brandy Station. And within a few weeks after the Rebel officers arrival in Richmond, devastating blows would be delivered to the South at Vicksburg, Port Hudson, and Gettysburg. These are but some of the reasons why the events of June 10, 1863 on the *Maple Leaf* have been eclipsed and all but forgotten.

Until recently, little regarding the escape has been generally available to the ever-growing number of Americans interested in the Civil War. It is, however, mentioned—though in briefest terms—in certain highly respected Civil War chronologies, as in

Moore's *Rebellion Record*, which has this to say under the heading of June 10, 1863:

> The Steamer Maple Leaf, en route from Fortress Monroe to Fort Delaware, with a large number of rebel prisoners, was taken possession of and run ashore about eight miles from Cape Henry Lighthouse, when a greater portion of the prisoners escaped.[41]

The *Civil War Almanac*, in its entry for that day described the event as an incident where an unspecified number of Confederate prisoners force the *Maple Leaf* ashore, and escape.[42] A similar entry is to be found in the *Civil War Day by Day*.[43]

The North Carolina Gazetteer: A Dictionary of Tar Heel Places, a principal source of information on North Carolina geography and history, explains that the town of Maple in Currituck County took its name from the ship, *Maple Leaf*, which ran aground nearby carrying 101 Confederate prisoners.[44]

The significance of the escape from the *Maple Leaf* is not that it was "one of the most daring acts of the war," as Asbury bragged, but that it is illustrative of the persistence of Southerners throughout the Confederacy, and their willingness to make sacrifices and take risks for their cause; a signal that, even in the summer of 1863, the war would not soon end, and that its last two years would be even bloodier than the first two.

Years later, A. E. Asbury searched unsuccessfully for others who had been aboard the *Maple Leaf* when it was captured. In March of 1886, he wrote of the event for the *St. Louis Republican*, expressing concern that the story would be forgotten, and ending the article:

> Having never seen an account of this brilliant act in print and never having met a participant since the war, I thought that I would after the lapse of twenty-three years, give you this plain statement and ask: 'Where are those gallant fellows? And who are left to tell this episode besides myself?'[45]

Perhaps this brief story would satisfy some of Asbury's concerns.

Notes

1. George G. Lewis and John Mewha, *History of Prisoner of War Utilization by the United States Army, 1776-1945*, Department of the Army Pamphlet 20-213 (Washington D.C.: GPO, 1955) p. 30, citing *The Reports of Committees of the House of Representatives Made During the Third Session of the Fortieth Congress, 1869* (Washington, D.C.: GPO, 1869), pp. 294, 335-61, 379-561.

2. NARA, CSR of Major James N. Wheelan, 1st Regiment of New York Mounted Rifles, RG 94.

3. Corcoran to Lincoln, August 17, 1863, allied papers with Record of Proceedings of Court of Inquiry. NARA, Records of The Office of The Judge Advocate General, RG 153.

4. A more accurate description of the place of General Corcoran's death places it at Sangster's Station, about four and one-half miles south south-west of Fairfax Court House (See *Atlas to OR*, plate 7.) *New York Times*, December 24, 1863. His funeral service, which filled St. Patrick's Cathedral in New York City, was attended by his old regiment, the 69th New York, as well as the 29th New York, and many dignitaries. Attendance was such as to require over 150 policemen to maintain order. *New York Times*, December 28, 1863.

5. Morris, *History of the Sixth New York Zouaves*, pp. 116-17.

6. NARA, CSR, William Wilson, 6th New York Infantry, RG 94.

7. NARA, CSR of William A. Dorsey, 3d Pennsylvania Artillery, RG 94. At the least, an inquiry might have made into the decision to mix prisoners supposedly paroled to good behavior with a larger group that had given no such assurances.

8. Telephone interview with Captain Oliver J. Semmes, III, USNR, October 1989. Since Semmes' resignation to join the Confederacy prevented his graduation from the Military Academy, he would have been pleased had he known that his grandson, Luke William Finlay, would graduate first in his West Point Class of 1928. *Register of Graduates and Former Cadets, United States Military Academy* (West Point, N.Y.: Association of Graduates, USMA, 1990), pp. 285-86, 395.

9. Oscar Haas, introductory comments to "The Diary of Julius Giesecke, 1863-1865," p. 27.

10. Taylor, *Destruction and Reconstruction*, p. 109.

11. Yeary, *Reminiscences*, pp. 674-75.

12. Goodspeed, *Central Arkansas*, pp. 744-45. With the end of Republican (Unionist) dominance in Arkansas, Col. Witt served in the 1874 constitutional convention which drafted the state's present, though often amended, constitution. Goodspeed, *Central Arkansas*, pp. 744-45. Fay Hempstead, *A Pictorial History*

of Arkansas From Earliest Times to the Year 1890 (St. Louis and New York: N. D. Thompson Publishing Co., 1890), pp. 644, 1215.

13. Whitten, introduction to *My Life in Prison and Escape. Tipton Weekly Record*, April 1906. *Confederate Veteran* 14 (May 1906): 227.

14. Josiah Royce, *California* (Boston and New York: Houghton, Mifflin and Company, 1886, repr. New York: AMS Press Inc., 1973), p. 449. Mary Floyd Williams, *History of the San Francisco Committee of Vigilance of 1851* (Berkeley, University of California Press, 1921), p. 177.

15. John Myers Myers, *San Francisco's Reign of Terror* (Garden City, N.Y.: Doubleday & Company, 1966), p. 283. This volume provides the most comprehensive account of the life of Edward "Med" McGowan, whose character was colorful enough to attract Myers to writing of a partly fictional "Med" McGowan in his novel, *I Jack Swilling* (New York: Hastings House, 1961).

16. Hoffman to Schoepf, July 15, 1863, *OR*, Series 2, vol. 6, p. 119.

17. Edward T. Downer, "Johnson's Island," *Civil War History* 8 (June 1962): 202-217.

18. [Buehring H. Jones], *Memorial of the Federal Prison on Johnson's Island, Lake Erie, Ohio, 1862-1864*, Collections of the Virginia Historical Society, 1887. The roll of prisoners included in this work contains several inaccurate entries.

19. Hoffman to Banks, *OR*, Series 2, vol. 7, p. 436. A. F. Wilson, "Would Not Surrender the Flag", *Confederate Veteran*, 10 (February 1902): 72.

20. *ORN*, Series 1, vol. 19, pp. 535-36.

21. Taylor, *Destruction and Reconstruction*, p. 135.

22. Asbury, *My Experiences*, pp. 26-27.

23. Richard S. Brownlee, *Gray Ghosts of the Confederacy - Guerilla Warfare in the West, 1861-1865* (Baton Rouge: Louisiana State University Press), p. 227.

24. Asbury, *My Experiences in the War*, p. 34. Apparently Asbury was unaware, or else unwilling to acknowledge, that one of his associates during his brief time under Anderson and Clements, was seventeen-year-old Jesse James, though at the time Asbury recorded his reminiscences, in 1892, the notorious outlaw had been dead for ten years. Clements was described by Asbury as a reasonable man who once saved his life, and who Asbury repaid with "a kindness" after the war. His description of Clements is in sharp contrast with others depicting him as a cold-blooded youth who enjoyed killing, and often scalped his victims. See *Spies, Scouts and Raiders*, "The Civil War," (Alexandria, Va.: Time-Life Publications, 1985), p. 159. For more on the Anderson Gang, Archie Clements, and Jesse James, see Brownlee, *Gray Ghosts*

of the Confederacy, pp. 230-46, and Donald R. Hale, *The Called Him Bloody Bill* (Clinton, Mo.: The Printery, 1975), pp. 83-99.

25. Asbury, "Capture of the Maple Leaf," 529.

26. Thomas R. Butchko, *On the Shores of the Pasquotank* (Elizabeth City: Museum of the Albemarle, 1989), p. 99. Richard B. Creecy, "Old Times in Betsy," *Elizabeth City Economist*, August 24, 1900.

27. Douglas Southall Freeman, *The South to Posterity: An Introduction to the Writing of Confederate History* (New York: Charles Scribner's Sons, 1951; repr., Wendell, NC: Broadfoot's Bookmark, 1983), p. 85.

28. Francis T. Miller, ed., *The Photographic History of the Civil War, Prisons and Hospitals* (New York: Review of Reviews, 1911), p. 173. Mary Chesnut, *Mary Chesnut's Civil War*, ed. C. Vann Woodward (New Haven and London: Yale University Press, 1981), p. 712.

29. Michael Corcoran, *The Captivity of General Corcoran* (Philadelphia: Barclay and Co, 1862), p. 29.

30. Lewis, *Seacoast Fortifications*, pp. 26, 28. Melchor, *Fort Norfolk*. Council on America's Military Past, *Headquarters Heliogram*, August 1991. Transcript of graffiti found at Fort Norfolk prepared by Marilyn S. Melchor and Debbie Brooks, August 1991, in files of author.

31. Joe Gray Taylor, *Louisiana Reconstructed, 1863-1877* (Baton Rouge: Louisiana State University Press, 1974), pp. 291-96.

32. Federal Writers' Project of the works Progress Administration, *New Orleans City Guide* (Boston: Houghton Mifflin Company, 1938), pp. 268-69.

33. Weinert, *Defender of the Chesapeake*, pp. 253-54.

34. Hoehling, *Last Days of the Confederacy*, pp. 5-6, 227-28, 236-38.

35. W. Emerson Wilson, *Fort Delaware* (Wilmington, Del.: Old Wilmington Printing Co., 1955; repr. William P. Frank, ed., Fort Delaware Historical Society, 1983).

36. Downer, "Johnson's Island," 202-217. Headquarters Heliogram, August 1991.

37. Heyl, *Early American Steamers*, vol. 5, pp. 283-84. A photograph of the *Cahawba* was recently displayed to millions of television viewers watching Ken Burns' production, *The Civil War*, which provided a view of the vessel as the narrator briefly described the Trent Affair, in which Confederate ambassadors Mason and Slidell, travelling to Europe from Nassau, were forcibly removed from the British steamer *Trent* by Captain Wilkes of the *U.S.S. San Jacinto*.

38. Heyl, *Early American Steamers*, vol. 1, pp. 65-66.

39. *The Philadelphia Inquirer*, April 13, 1864. *New York Times*, April 13, 1864. *Cleveland Plain Dealer*, April 15, 1864. *Civil War News*, October 1991.

40. Edwin C. Bearss, Chief Historian, United States Department of the Interior, National Park Service, quoted in Keith V. Holland, Lee B. Manley, and James W. Towart, eds. *The Maple Leaf - An Extraordinary American Civil War Shipwreck* (Jacksonville, Fla.: St. Johns Archaeological Expeditions, Inc., 1993). This work provides a detailed history of the ship, covering its construction and time as a great lakes steamer in Canada, its service during the Civil War, and its eventual destruction. Also provided are descriptions of the present-day wreck, and techniques employed (as well as problems encountered) in recovering artifacts.

41. Frank Moore, ed., *The Rebellion Record: A Diary of American Events, with Documents, Narratives, Illustrative Incidents, Poetry, Etc.* (New York: D. Van Nostrand, 1861-1871), vol. 7, p. 6. Despite its brevity, the most comprehensive account of the event is J. L. Bryan's "The Maple Leaf Affair," in *Confederate Veteran* (Jan. - Feb. 1993): 20-25.

42. John S. Bowman, ed., *Civil War Almanac* (New York: World Almanac Publications, 1983), s.v. "June 10, 1863."

43. E. B. Long and Barbara Long, *The Civil War Day By Day - An Almanac, 1861-1865* (Garden City, NY: Doubleday, 1971), p. 364.

44. William S. Powell, *The North Carolina Gazetteer: A Dictionary of Tar Heel Places* (Chapel Hill, N.C.: University of North Carolina Press, 1968), s.v. Maple.

45. Asbury, *My Experiences*, p. 22. *Elizabeth City Economist*, August 18, 1899. Asbury later did meet one of the veterans of the *Maple Leaf*, Captain Samuel S. Asbury, of Farmington, Missouri, not a relative. Asbury, "Capture of the Maple Leaf," 529.

Appendix A

Roster

Confederate Prisoners on Board the *Maple Leaf*, June 10, 1863.

Name, Grade and Organization	Group	Escape

(NOG = New Orleans Group; FNG = Fort Norfolk Group)

1.	Alston, Samuel, 1LT, Crescent Regiment captured at Butte a la Rose, Sept 20, 1863, resident of New Orleans.	NOG	Yes
2.	Andrews, W. H., 1LT, 1st Ala.	NOG	Yes
3.	Asbury, Ai Edgar, CPT, 6th Mo. Cav, captured at West Plains, Howell County, Mo., Apr 20, 1863, resident of Houston, Texas County, Mo.	FNG	No
4.	Asbury, Samuel L., 1LT, 45th Miss., captured at Murfreesboro, January 5, 1863, resident of Salem, Miss.; after the war Farmington, Mo. Among the wounded on the *Maple Leaf*.	FNG	No
5.	Atkinson, J. J., CPT, Gunboat *Hart*.	NOG	Yes
6.	Balch, Charles, 1LT, 45th CSA, captured in Shelby County, Tenn., April 16, 1863.	FNG	Yes
7.	Bast, William A., 2LT, Co B, 3d Mo. Cav, captured in Stoddard County, Mo., April 30, 1863, paroled March 9, 1864, resident of Loutre Island, Montgormery County, Mo.	FNG	No
8.	Beard, Travis R., 1LT, Co F, 24th Tex. Cav, captured at Arkansas Post, January 11, 1863, resident of Big Creek, Tex, age 26.	FNG	No
9.	Bell, W. M., 2LT, 3d Tenn. Cav, captured April 4, 1863, Berne Post, resident of Rome, Tenn.	FNG	No

	Name, Grade and Organization	Group	Escape
10.	Brown, T. N., 1LT, Lee Battery.	NOG	Yes
11.	Broyles, B. F., 1LT, 7th Tex. Cav.	NOG	Yes
12.	Brugnions, A. G., 1LT, Co E, Crescent Regt, captured at Butte La Rose, April 20, 1863.	NOG	Yes
13.	Camford, C. L., 1LT, 11th La. Cav.	NOG	Yes
14.	Campbell, Stephen, 2LT, 6th [5th] Mo. Cav, captured in Howard County, Mo., Jan 4, 1863.	FNG	NO
15.	Cannon, Wynne G., 1LT, 154th Tenn, captured at Murfreesboro, January 5, 1863.	FNG	Yes
16.	Carmouche, E. A., 1LT, 4th La.	NOG	Yes
17.	Coffee, Hiram, 2LT, Co I, 1st TN Legion	FNG	No
18.	Covington, C. D., 1LT, Co B, 45th Tenn., captured at Franklin, Tenn., April 27, 1863, resident of Daingerfield, Tex.	FNG	No
19.	Crath, D. T., CPT, Gen Beauregard's staff.	NOG	Yes
20.	Dougherty, James H., LTC, 5th Mo. Cav, captured in Jackson County, Mo., April 26, 1863.	FNG	Yes
21.	Downing, John F., CPT, Steams Regt, captured March 15, 1863.	FNG	Yes
22.	Dubecq, J., 1LT, Gunboat *Diana*.	NOG	Yes
23.	Duff, William H., CPT, 3d Brigade, CSA, captured in Green County.	FNG	Yes
24.	Estes, David N., 1LT, 9th Tenn Cav (Bn), captured near Baton Rouge, 1863.	NOG	Yes
25.	Fisk, H. L., 1LT, Gen. Beauregard's Staff.	NOG	Yes

	Name, Grade and Organization	Group	Escape
26.	Francis, T. H., CPT, Co A, 4th Tenn., wounded and captured at Murfreesboro, Tenn. January 5, 1863, resident of Memphis, Tenn.	FNG	No
27.	Fuller, Emelius W., CPT, formerly of the St. Martin (La.) Rangers, and commander of the *Cotton*, captured at Bayou Teche, April 14, 1863 with the destruction of his ship, *Queen of the West*, died at Johnson's Island, July 25, 1863.	NOG	No
28.	Fusilier, G. Leclerc, CPT, ADC on Gen Richard Taylor's Staff, captured at Irish Bend, April 15, 1863, resident of St. Mary's Parish, La.	NOG	Yes
29.	Giesecke, Julius, CPT, 4th Tex. Cav, captured at Irish Bend, La., April 14, 1863, resident of New Braunfels, Tex.	NOG	Yes
30.	Gilbeau, Charles, 1LT, 30th La.	NOG	Yes
31.	Green, G., 2LT, Cox's Tenn. Cav, captured in Shelby County, Tenn., April 16, 1863.	FNG	Yes
32.	Green, John Uriah, LTC, 12th Tenn., captured in Shelby County, Tenn., April 16, 1863.	FNG	Yes
33.	Griffin, Benjamin, CPT, Co F, 1st Tex. Legion, captured at Franklin, 27 April 1863, resident of Clarksville, Tenn.	FNG	No
34.	Hendley, Henry M., 2LT, Burstbridge Regt, captured in Stoddard County, Mo., April 20, 1863.	FNG	No
35.	Hicks, F. Y., 1LT, Co B, 49th N.C., captured in Craven County [Sandridge], N.C., April 21, 1863, resident of Camp Call, N.C.	FNG	No
36.	Hicks, Felix D., 2LT, 1st Tenn., captured at McMinville, April 21, 1863.	FNG	Yes

	Name, Grade and Organization	Group	Escape
37.	Hinson, Joseph, 1LT, Co A, Miles' Legion captured at Greenville Springs, La., May 2, 1863.	NOG	Yes
38.	Holloway, George W., CPT, 11th La. (Bn), captured on Grand Lake, April 14, 1863, with destruction of *Queen of the West*.	NOG	Yes
39.	Holmes, Eugene, CPT, Co E, Crescent Regt, captured Franklin, La., April 14, 1863.	NOG	Yes
40.	Hughes, David M. C., 1LT, Co A and D, Miles Legion, captured at Port Hudson, La., May 21, 1863.	NOG	Yes
41.	Jackson, Andrew, 2LT, Carroll's Cav, in Crawford County, Ark., March 17, 1863.	FNG	Yes
42.	Jackson, R. Stark, 1LT, Co I, F, and S, 8th La., age 18, resident of Cheneyville, La.	NOG	Yes
43.	Jeter, William G., 1LT, Co F, 4th La., enlisted May 25, 1861, Tangipahoa, La., killed at battle of Poor House, July 28, 1864.	NOG	Yes
44.	Jones, W. [H.] S., 2LT, Co I, 2d Ark., captured at Murfreesboro, December 31, 1862.	FNG	No
45.	Kelsey, Samuel W., 1LT, 10th Ark., captured at Port Hudson, May 27, 1863.	NOG	Yes
46.	Kirkland, J. D., 1LT, 9th La.	NOG	Yes
47.	Lewis, Gabriel, 2LT, Co A, 9th Ky., captured at Murfreesboro, Jan 9, 1863.	FNG	Yes
48.	Lilley, Wm. H., 1LT, 10th Ark., captured at Port Hudson, May 27, 1863.	NOG	Yes
49.	Locke, H. A., 1LT, Co K, 30th Miss., captured at Murfreesboro, January 9, 1863, resident of Canton, Tenn.	FNG	No

	Name, Grade and Organization	Group	Escape
50.	Long, J. H., CPT, 4th Tex. Cav, captured at Irish Bend, La., April 14, 1863, age 26.	NOG	Yes
51.	Lynn, David A., CPT, Co F, 18th Va. Cav, captured in Hampshire County [Hampson], Va., March 11, 1863, resident of Cumberland, Md.	FNG	No
52.	McClain, Frank Jay, CPT, Co A, 9th Tenn., resident of Columbia, Tenn.	NOG	No
53.	McDonald, D. M., 1LT, Co B, 56th N.C., captured at Gum [Green] Swamp, N.C., May 22, 1863, resident of Fayetteville, N.C.	FNG	No
54.	McGowan, Edward, carried on Federal rolls as Purser of the gunboat *Diana*.	NOG	Yes
55.	McSpaddin, Benjamin J., CPT, 1st Tenn., captured in Shelby County, Tenn., May 12, 1863.	FNG	Yes
56.	Martin, B. F., 2LT, Co D, 25th Tex. Cav, captured at Arkansas Post, resident of Goliad, Tex.	FNG	No
57.	Mathews, Ludwick, CPT, Co D and I, 15th Ark., captured Fort Donelson February 16, 1862, exchanged November 8, 1862; captured near Port Hudson, May 28, 1863.	NOG	Yes
58.	Melburne, W. E., 1LT, 27th N.C., captured in Berlin County, January 4, 1863.	FNG	Yes
59.	Melville, Thomas D., 1LT, Co H, 18th La., captured April 13, 1863, Franklin, La., paroled at Shreveport, La., June 21, 1865.	NOG	Yes
60.	Mobley, J. M., 1LT, 1st Choctaw Bn.	NOG	Yes
61.	Morrison, J. A., 1LT, 50th N.C., captured at Rodmans Point, N.C., April 16, 1863.	FNG	Yes

Name, Grade and Organization	Group	Escape
62. Morse, A. Porter., 1LT, Ordnance Corps, captured at Alexandria, La., May 12, 1863, ADC to Brig. Gen. J. P. Major.	NOG	Yes
63. Moss, Thomas E., 1LT, 2d Ky., captured at Murfreesboro, April 9, 1863, later attorney general of Kentucky.	FNG	Yes
64. Musselman, James M., 1LT, Co A, 4th La., captured Baton Rouge, La., February 10, 1863, sent from Fort Monroe to Fort Delaware June 13, 1863, to Johnson's Island July 20, 1863, died October 20, 1863.	NOG	No
65. Nation, David A., 1LT, Co E, 15th Ark., near Port Hudson, May 28, 1863.	NOG	Yes
66. Nelson, William S., 1LT, Co E, Crescent Regt, captured Butte a la Rose, April 20, 1863.	NOG	Yes
67. Noland, Robert C., 2LT, 1st CSA Cav, captured in Tenn., January 22, 1863.	FNG	Yes
68. Parker, Edward S., CPT, 50th N.C., captured at . . . port, N.C., April 16, 1863.	FNG	Yes
69. Porter, J. M., 1LT, Ariz. Bn, captured while on picket duty near Opelousas in connection with operations at Irish Bend, April 1863.	NOG	Yes
70. Pruett, William Henry, CPT, Co I, 1st Ala., captured near Port Hudson, May 20, 1863.	NOG	Yes
71. Richardson, I. A., CPT, 62d Ga., captured near Washington, N.C., April 19, 1863.	FNG	Yes
72. Riddings, G. D., 1LT, Co A, 11th [10th] Tenn., captured at Murfreesboro, January 5, 1863, resident of Maberly, Tenn.	FNG	No
73. Roby, F. M., LT, CS Navy, captured at Fort Hindeman (Arkansas Post), January 11, 1863.	FNG	Yes

	Name, Grade and Organization	Group	Escape
74.	Rogers, W. H., 1LT, Co K & E, Crescent Regt, captured Butte a la Rose, La., April 20, 1863, paroled Natchitoches, La., June 6, 1865.	NOG	Yes
75.	Roussell, Charles, 1LT, Co H, 10th La., captured March 25, 1863, at Bonnet Carre, La., resident of St John the Baptist Parish, La., occupation Planter, age 24, single.	NOG	Yes
76.	Schlick, Albert F., 1LT, Co G, "The Dutch Co." 4th Tex. Cav, wounded and captured at Irish Bend, La., April 14, 1863, resident of Gonzales, Tex., age 23.	NOG	Yes
77.	Scott, E. A., CPT, 9th La. (Bn)	NOG	Yes
78.	Seckel, Richard Twells, CPT, Jeff Thompson's Bde, captured at Bloomfield, Mo., Apr 20, 1863, resident of Paris, Tex.	FNG	Yes
79.	Semmes, Oliver J., CPT, 1st CSA Light Arty Btry, captured with the destruction of the gunboat *Diana* at Irish Bend, Apr 1863.	NOG	Yes
80.	Sibley, W. L., 2LT, Co K, 25th La., wounded and captured at Murfreesboro, Tenn., January 4, 1863, taken from Fort Monroe to Fort Delaware June 13, 1863, to Johnson's Island, to City Point for exchange February 16, 1865, paroled at Marion, Ala., May 15, 1865, resident of Lake Providence, La.	FNG	No
81.	Smith, Frank J., 1LT, 1st Mo. Cav, captured at Jefferson County, Mo., April 25, 1863. Sent from St. Louis toward City Point, June 5, 1863, age 36.	FNG	Yes
82.	Smith, John M., 1LT, Helms Co., Herberts Bn, AZ Cav (1st Tex.-Ariz. Bn of Mounted Rifles).	NOG	Yes

	Name, Grade and Organization	Group	Escape
83.	Stafford, George W., 1LT, Co I, 8th La., captured at Alexandria, La., May 12, 1863, resident of Cheneyville, La., student at enlistment, age 16, transferred to Gen. Stafford's staff Feb 1864.	NOG	Yes
84.	Strong, Jno., 2LT, Fielder's Mo. Home Guards, captured at Stoddard County, Mo., March 26, 1863.	FNG	No
85.	Swain, W. C., 2LT, Co F, 1st Tex., captured at Franklin, La. (Irish Bend), April 27, 1863.	FNG	Yes
86.	Thornton, R. W., 1LT, Co B, 56th N.C., captured at Gum Swamp, NC, May 22 [27], 1863, resident of Fayetteville, NC.	FNG	No
87.	Watkins, J. M., 2LT, Fowler's Cav, captured in Harrum County, Ark., June 20, 1862.	FNG	Yes
88.	Webre, John, Jr., 1LT, Co H, 28th (Thomas') La., captured at Baton Rouge, LA, February 16, 1863, paroled November 1, 1865, resident of Napoleonville, Parish of Assumption, La.	NOG	Yes
89.	Welsh, William, 1LT, Bury's Co., Herberts Bn, AZ Cav (1st Tex.-Ariz. Bn of Mounted Rifles).	NOG	Yes
90.	Wilkinson, H. W., 1LT, Steede's Bn.	NOG	Yes
91.	Williams, Levi Bronson, 1LT, Co E, 63d N.C., captured in Ostow County, N.C., March 8, 1863, resident of N.C., died at Johnston's Island, September 29, 1863.	FNG	No
92.	Williamson, J., 2LT, Franklin's Cav, captured in Cairo County, April 20, 1863.	FNG	Yes
93.	Wilson, James H., CPT, 11th Ky. Cav, captured at Morris Station, April 21, 1863.	FNG	Yes

	Name, Grade and Organization	Group	Escape
94.	Witmore, John, 1LT, N.C. Battery (2d NC Arty), Captured at Gum Springs, May 22, 1863, released on parole July 1863, resident of Cumberland Cy.	FNG	No
95.	Witt, Allen R., COL, 10th Ark., captured at Port Hudson, May 27, 1863, resident of Quitman, Ark.	NOG	Yes
96.	Wolf, John B., CPT, 14th Ark., captured near Port Hudson, 1863.	NOG	Yes
97.	Youngblood, J. W., CPT, Gen. Gardner's Staff (Signal Corps), captured at Port Hudson, resident of Memphis, Tenn.	NOG	No

Appendix B

A Note on Exchanges and Paroles

Early during the war, the North and South routinely exchanged prisoners, normally on a one for one basis, because it was considered the humane thing to do and a mark of "civilized warfare." The protocol, negotiated by Major Generals John A. Dix and Daniel H. Hill on July 22, 1862, provided specific rules and "equivalents" for purpose of exchange. Thus, a colonel could be exchanged for fifteen privates, a brigadier general for twenty, and so on.[1]

In the event the opposing forces had no prisoners immediately available for exchange, or exchange was for other reasons impracticable, either side might nonetheless release a prisoner on his parole, or oath, that he would not engage in hostilities against his former captors until such time as he should be "exchanged."

Each side kept careful records of prisoners released on parole pending exchange. The system was administered by officials known as agents of exchange, who, in the summer of 1863, were Lieutenant Colonel William H. Ludlow at Fort Monroe and Colonel Robert Ould at Richmond. These men would, from time to time, agree that a certain number of Union soldiers paroled by a Confederate commander would be considered exchanged for a specific number of Confederate soldiers paroled by a Union officer. After these "paper" exchanges, the paroled soldiers were declared free to resume hostilities.

Releasing prisoners on parole had benefits for both sides. For the prisoner these are obvious, but for his captor, they are also significant. In some situations, such as a raid into enemy territory, the capturing army was not equipped to take prisoners, and had little choice but to release them on parole. Most importantly, paroles relieved armies of the burden of guarding, feeding, and otherwise providing for prisoners who consumed their resources. An example is the parole by Confederate authorities of 1,600 U.S. soldiers captured at Shiloh, "in consequence of [the Confederates] being unable to feed them."[2]

The system of paroles and exchanges benefited thousands of soldiers on both sides, sparing them the discomfort, disease, and often death suffered in facilities that were never intended to hold the large number of prisoners that were packed into them, particularly toward the end of the war.

The foundation of the system, however, the Dix-Hill Protocol, was a source of endless controversy. Some officers complained that their men would invite capture, knowing that they would be paroled and thus avoid the dangers of combat.

An example of these controversies occurred when General Henry Halleck, the Union General in Chief, chastised General Banks for paroling the soldiers of Confederate General Franklin Gardner's command, surrendered at Port Hudson. Halleck claimed that releases on exchange or parole could only take place at the designated locations, Vicksburg and City Point, as specified in the cartel, which was always strictly construed. He agreed that the designated locations could be changed by agreement of the commanders of the opposing armies, but insisted that any modification must have been entered into while General Gardner was able to act independently—meaning before he had surrendered—rather than afterwards, which was what occurred.

Confederate Commissioner Ould also argued that the paroles were invalid, but on other grounds. He agreed with Halleck, that the designated locations could be modified by the commanders of *opposing Armies* (italics added), but contended that General Gardner at Port Hudson was a subordinate of Lieutenant General Pemberton, at Vicksburg, and had no such authority. There were countless other similar squabbles dealing with interpretations of the protocol, and it is a wonder that so many men were released.

Informal paroles of the type given by the men of the Norfolk group, and later by Lieutenant Dorsey and the officers of the *Maple Leaf*, had a tenuous legal basis. Colonel William Winthrop, the preeminent scholar of military law of the period, does not discuss such a concept. The notion was, however, mentioned by the Union Army's General Orders Number 207, curiously—and suspiciously—published on July 3, 1863, just days after the escape from the *Maple Leaf*:

> A military parole not to serve until exchanged must not be confounded with a parole of honor to do or

not to do a particular thing not inconsistent with the duty of a soldier. *Thus, a prisoner of war actually held by the enemy may, in order to obtain exemption from a close guard or confinement, pledge his parole of honor that he will make no attempt to escape. Such pledges are binding upon the individuals giving them; but they should seldom be given or received, for it is the duty of a prisoner to escape if able to do so.* [Italics added.] Any pledge or parole of honor extorted from a prisoner by ill-usage or cruelty is not binding.[3]

So, it could be argued that the informal paroles of the type given by Green and his associates in St. Louis, and by Lieutenant Dorsey in promising not to return to Fort Monroe, though not specified in the cartel, nevertheless had some basis in customary usage during the Civil War.

Notes

1. See enclosure to Dix to Stanton, July 23, 1862, *OR*, Series 2, vol. 3, p. 266, a transcript of which follows this section.

2. Winthrop, *Military Law and Precedent*, p. 791, citing Moore, *Rebellion Record*, 5: 23.

3. War Department, Washington D. C., Adjutant General's Office, General Orders No. 207, July 3, 1863, *OR*, Series 2, vol. 6, pp. 78-79. For a discussion of the doctrine of paroles and exchanges generally, see Winthrop, *Military Law and Precedent*, p. 793, et. seq. The decline in use of prisoner exchanges during the later part of the war, is discussed by Lewis and Mewha in *History of Prisoner of War Utilization*. See also, Francis Trevelyan Miller, ed., *The Photographic History of the Civil War*, (New York: Review of Reviews, 1911), vol. 4, *Prisons and Hospitals*, by Holland Thompson, pp. 98-122. The most extensive and best treatment of the subject is William Best Hesseltine's *Civil War Prisons - A Study in War Psychology* (Columbus, Ohio: The Ohio State University Press, 1930).

Enclosure to Appendix B

The Dix-Hill Cartel

Headquarters, Fort Monroe, VA., July 23, 1862

Hon. E. M. Stanton, *Secretary of War*
SIR: I have the honor to inclose the articles of agreement entered into by Maj. Gen. D. H. Hill and myself for a general exchange of prisoners of war.
I am, very respectfully, yours,
JOHN A. DIX
Major-General

[Inclosure.]

Haxall's Landing, on James River, Va.,
July 22, 1862

The undersigned having been commissioned by the authorities they respectively represent to make arrangements for a general exchange of prisoners of war have agreed to the following articles:

ART. 1. It is hereby agreed and stipulated that all prisoners of war held by either party including those taken on private armed vessels known as privateers shall be discharged upon the conditions and term following:
Prisoners to be exchanged man for man and officers for officer; privateers to be placed upon the footing of officers and men of the Navy.
Men and officers of lower grades may be exchanged for officers of a higher grade, and men and officers of different services may be exchanged according to the following scale of equivalents:
A general commanding in chief or an admiral shall be exchanged for officers of equal rank, or for sixty privates or common seamen.

A flag officer or major-general shall be exchanged for officers of equal rank, or for forty privates or common seamen.

A commodore carrying a broad pennant or a brigadier-general shall be exchanged for officers of equal rank, or twenty privates or common seamen.

A captain in the Navy or a colonel shall be exchanged for officers of equal rank, or for fifteen privates or common seamen.

A lieutenant-colonel or a commander in the Navy shall be exchanged for officers of equal rank, or for ten privates or common seamen.

A lieutenant-commander or a major shall be exchanged for officers of equal rank, or eight privates or common seamen.

A lieutenant or master in the Navy or a captain in the Army or marines shall be exchanged for officers of equal rank, or six privates or common seamen.

Master's mates in the Navy or lieutenants and ensigns in the Army shall be exchanged for officers of equal rank, or four privates or common seamen.

Midshipmen, warrant officers in the Navy, masters of merchant vessels and commanders of privateers shall be exchanged for officers of equal rank, or three privates or common seamen.

Second captain, lieutenants or mates of merchant vessels or privateers and all petty officers in the Navy and all non-commissioned officers in the Army or marines shall be severally exchanged for persons of equal rank, or for two privates or common seamen, and private soldiers or common seamen shall be exchanged for each other, man for man.

ART. 2. Local State, civil and militia rank held by persons not in actual military service will not be recognized, the basis of exchange being the grade actually held in the naval and military service of the respective parties.

ART. 3. If citizens held by either party on charges of disloyalty or any alleged civil offense are exchanged it shall only be for citizens. Captured sutlers, teamsters and all civilians in the actual service of either party to be exchanged for persons in similar position.

ART. 4. All prisoners of war to be discharged on parole in ten days after their capture, and the prisoners now held and those hereafter taken to be transported to the points mutually agreed upon at the expense of the capturing party. The surplus prisoners not exchanged shall not be permitted to take up arms again, nor to serve as military police or constabulary force in any fort, garrison or field work held by either of the respective parties, nor as guards of prisons, depots or stores, nor to discharge any duty usually performed by soldiers, until exchanged under the provisions of this cartel. The exchange is not to be considered complete until the officer or soldier exchanged for has been actually restored to the lines to which he belongs.

ART. 5. Each party upon the discharge of prisoners of the other party is authorized to discharge an equal number of their own officers or men from parole, furnishing at the same time to the other party a list of their prisoners discharged and of their own officers and men relieved from parole, thus enabling each party to relieve from parole such of their own officers and men as the party may choose. The lists thus mutually furnished will keep both parties advised of the true condition of the exchange of prisoners.

ART. 6. The stipulations and provisions above mentioned to be of binding obligation during the continuance of the war, it matters not which party may have the surplus of prisoners, the great principles involved being, first, and equitable exchange of prisoners, man for man, officer for officer, or officer of higher grade exchanged for officers of lower grade or for privates, according to the scale of equivalents; second, that privateers and officers and men of different services may be exchanged according to the same scale of equivalents; third, that all prisoners, of whatever arm of service, are to be exchanged or paroled in ten days from the time of their capture, if it be practicable to transfer them to their own lines in that time; if not, as soon thereafter as practicable; fourth, that no officer, soldier or employee, in the service of their party is to be considered as exchanged and absolved from his parole until his equivalent has actually reached the lines of his friends; fifth, that the parole forbids the performance of field, garrison, police, or guard, or constabulary duty.

JOHN A. DIX
Major-General

D. H. HILL
Major-General, C. S. Army

SUPPLEMENTARY ARTICLES

ART. 7. All prisoners of war now held on either side and all prisoners hereafter taken shall be sent with all reasonable dispatch to A. M. Aiken's, below Dutch Gap, on the James River, Va.,[1] or to Vicksburg, on the Mississippi River, in the State of Mississippi, and there exchanged or paroled until such exchange can be effected, notice being previously given by each party of the number of prisoners it will send and the time when they will be delivered at those points respectively; and in case the vicissitudes of war shall change the military relations of the places designated in this article to the contending parties so as to render the same inconvenient for the delivery and exchange of prisoners, other places bearing as nearly as may be the present local relations of said places to the lines of said parties shall be by mutual agreement substituted. But nothing in this article contained shall prevent the commanders of two opposing armies from exchanging prisoners or releasing them on parole from other points mutually agreed on by said commanders.

ART. 8. For the purpose of carrying into effect the foregoing articles of agreement each party will appoint two agents, to be called agents for the exchange of prisoners of war, whose duty it shall be to communicate with each other by correspondence and otherwise, to prepare and lists of prisoners, to attend to the delivery of the prisoners at the places agreed on and to carry out promptly, effectually and in good faith all the details and provisions of the said articles of agreement.

113

ART. 9. And in case any misunderstanding shall arise in regard to any clause or stipulation in the foregoing articles it is mutually agreed that such misunderstanding shall not interrupt the release of prisoners on parole, as herein provided, but shall be made the subject of friendly explanations in order that the object of this agreement may neither be defeated nor postponed.

JOHN A. DIX
Major-General

D. H. HILL
Major-General, C. S. Army

Notes

1. Later changed to nearby City Point, Va., also on the James River.

Appendix C

Lieutenant Colonel Ludlow's Report

Head Quarters, Department of Va.
Seventh Army Corps
Fort Monroe, June 12th 1863

Major General John A. Dix
Commanding Department of Va.

General,

In compliance with your instructions, I have investigated the circumstances of the escape of rebel officers from the Steamer Maple Leaf, and have the honor to report that the steamer left Fort Monroe at half past one, on the afternoon of Wednesday, the 10th instant for Fort Delaware with ninety seven Confederate officers prisoners of war.

Of this number forty seven had given their paroles to commit no act of hostility against the United States, until regularly exchanged.

The boat and prisoners were under the charge of Lt. Wm E. Dorsey, 3d Regt. Penna. Arty. with the usual guard.

After proceeding about two hours, Cape Henry light house, bearing south about six miles distant, a few of the Confederate officers led by Edward McGowan, purser of the Gun Boat Diana, seized the arms of the guard & took possession of the steamer.

It appears in evidence that the paroled officers were opposed to the act, and had Lieut. Dorsey with his guard properly performed their duties, they would have had the aid and cooperation of these paroled officers to preserve discipline and order.

<u>The muskets of the guard were not loaded.</u>

The Sergeant of the Guard states that he had received no order to load them. Lt. Dorsey admits that he did not know, whether they were loaded or not, and had made no inspection at any time of them. The guard had received from their Commanding Officer no instructions as to their duties.

It appears also in evidence that this neglect of duty was observed and commented on by those who rose upon the guard and invited the rising.

After taking possession of the steamer it was determined to proceed to Nassau N.P. but finding upon examination that there was not coal enough to enable them to reach that port, the steamer was stopped about eight miles south of Cape Henry Light House, and a half a mile from shore and all the prisoners, excepting twenty seven escaped in the boats to the shore. Among those who escaped were twenty three officers who had given their parole as above mentioned.

It is due to them however to state that they were not in the original plot. The determination of the twenty seven officers not to leave the steamer in all probability saved her from burning.

I enclose to you their names. They have this day been sent to Fort Delaware.

An oath was exacted from the officers of the steamer and from Lt Dorsey and his guard that they would proceed direct to Fort Delaware and give no information of what had occurred, until after their arrival at that post.

The boat was however, brought back to Fort Monroe and arrived here about midnight. Lt. Dorsey reported to me about nine o'clock on the morning of the 11th inst. and I immediately in your absence at Williamsburg, telegraphed necessary orders to General Peck and General Viele to send out cavalry and other forces to intercept the fugitives who had arranged to go in the direction of Elizabeth City.

In the course of the investigation I have examined Capt. H. W. Dale, John Carmine, Pilot, W. A Smith, Engineer, C. H. Farnham, mate all officers of the Maple Leaf. Also Captain Fuller, Captain Youngblood, and Lieut. Witmore, prisoners of war and who were among the twenty seven officers who refused to leave the steamer.

Also Lt. Wm. E. Dorsey and Thomas B. Bernie, Sergeant of the guard.

The testimony though somewhat confused, has not been conflicting.

I am very respectfully
Wm H. Ludlow
Lt Col & Inspector Genl
7th Army Corps

Bibliography

Newspapers

Boston Daily Advertiser, 1863.
Cleveland Plain Dealer, 1864.
Daily Richmond Examiner, 1863.
Elizabeth City Economist, 1899.
New Orleans Daily Picayune, 1863.
New York Herald, 1863.
New York Times, 1856, 1857, 1863, 1864.
New York Daily Tribune, 1863.
Philadelphia Inquirer, 1863, 1864.
Richmond Enquirer, 1863.
San Francisco Alta California, 1863.
Washington Evening Star, 1863.

Published Primary Sources

Asbury, Ai Edgar. *My Experiences in the War 1861 to 1865*. Kansas City, Mo.: Berkowitz & Co., 1894.

——"Capture of the Maple Leaf." *Confederate Veteran* 6 (November 1898): 529.

Chesnutt, Mary. *Mary Chestnut's Civil War*. Edited by C. Vann Woodward. New Haven and London: Yale University Press, 1981.

Corcoran, Michael. *The Captivity of General Corcoran*. Philadelphia: Barclay and Co, 1862.

Fremantle, Arthur James Lyon. *The Fremantle Diary*. Edited by Walter Lord. Boston: Little, Brown and Company, 1954.

Gibson, Thomas R. "Gen. James H. McBride." *Confederate Veteran* 23 (August 1915): 375.

Haas, Oscar, trans. and ed. "Diary of Julius Giesecke, 1863-1865." *Texas Military History*, 4 (Spring 1964): 27-54.

Green, John Uriah. *My Life in Prison and Escape: A Story of the Civil War*. Edited by J. G. Whitten. Navasota, Tex: Navasota Examiner-Review, 1952.

Hollowell, Mrs. Cristopher W. "The Maple Leaf." *Elizabeth City Economist*, September 1, 1899.

Jones, John B. *A Rebel War Clerk's Diary*. Edited by Earl Schenck Miers. New York: Sagamore Press, Inc. Publications, 1958.

Kendall, John Smith, ed. "Recollections of a Confederate Officer," (John Irwin Kendall). *The Louisiana Historical Quarterly* 29 (October 1946): 1041-1141.

Morse, A. Porter. "The Capture of the Maple Leaf." Edited by William Rand Browne. *The Southern Magazine*, September 1871, pp. 302-09.

Taylor, Richard. *Destruction and Reconstruction: Personal Experiences of the Late War*. New York: D. Appleton and Company, 1879.

U.S. Navy Department. *Official Records of the Union and Confederate Navies in the War of the Rebellion*. 26 vols. Washington, D.C.: GPO, 1894-1922.

U.S. War Department. *The War of the Rebellion: A Compilation of the Official Records of the Union and Confederate Armies*. 130 vols. Washington, D.C.: GPO, 1880-1901.

—— *Atlas to Accompany the Official Records of the Union and Confederate Armies*. Calvin Cowles, comp., Washington, D.C.: GPO, 1891-1895; repr. ed., New York: Fairfax Press, 1983.

Wilson, A. F. "Would Not Surrender the Flag: Reminiscences of the Queen of the West." *Confederate Veteran* 10 (February 1902): 72.

Wolf, John B. "Capture of the Maple Leaf." *Confederate Veteran* 29 (October 1921): 375.

Yeary, Mamie, comp. *Reminiscences of the Boys in Gray (1861-1865)*. Dallas: Smith and Lamar, 1912.

Unpublished Primary Sources

McHorney, Edmond. *How the Officers Escaped*. Reminiscences of Edmond McHorney, Coinjock, NC, unpublished manuscript in possession of J. Rives Manning, Jr., Roanoke Rapids, N.C.

National Archives and Records Administration. Washington, D.C. Military Records of Soldiers Who Served During the Civil War, Records of the Adjutant General's Office, Department of War, Record Group 94; War Department Collection of Confederate Records, Compiled Service Records of Confederate Soldiers Who Served During the Civil War, Record Group 109; Records of the Office of The Judge Advocate General, Department of War, Record Group 153.

Secondary Sources and Refrences

Association of Graduates, U.S. Military Academy. *Register of Graduates and Former Cadets*. West Point, N.Y. Assocaition of Graduates, 1990.

Basler, Roy P., ed. *The Collected Works of Abraham Lincoln*. New Brunswick, N.J.: Rutgers University Press, 1953. Vol. 5.

Beers, Henry Putney. *Guide to the Archives of the Government of the Confederate States of America*. National Archives Publication No. 68-15. Washington, D.C.: GPO, 1968.

Bergeron, Arthur W., Jr. *Guide to Louisiana Confederate Military Units, 1861-1865*. Baton Rouge and London: Louisiana State University Press, 1989.

Biographical and Historical Memoirs of Central Arkansas. Chicago, Nashville, and St. Louis: The Goodspeed Publishing Co., 1889; repr. Easley, S.C.: Southern Historical Press, 1978.

Booth, Andrew B., comp. *Records of Louisiana Confederate Soldiers and Louisiana Confederate Commands*. New Orleans: 1928, repr. Spartanburg, S.C.: The Reprint Company, Publishers, 1984.

Bowman, John S., ed. *The Civil War Almanac*. With an introduction by Henry Steele Commager. New York: World Almanac Publications, 1983.

Browne, W. B. "Stranger than Fiction: Capture of United States Steamer Maple Leaf, Near Cape Henry, Half a Century Ago," *Southern Historical Society Papers*, 39 (April 1914): 181-85.

Brownlee, Richard S. *Gray Ghosts of the Confederacy: Guerrilla Warfare in the West, 1861-1865*. Baton Rouge: Louisiana State University Press, 1958.

Bryan, J. L. "The Maple Leaf Affair," *Confederate Veteran* (January-February 1993): 20-25.

Butchko, Thomas R. *On the Shores of the Pasquotank*. Elizabeth City: Museum of the Albemarle, 1989.

Confederate Veteran. "My Experiences in the War of 1861-1864." Note regarding narrative of Ai Edgar Asbury, 20 (May 1912): 242.

Confederate Veteran. "Prison Life and Escape of Col. Green." Note summarizing narrative of Col. Green, 7 (January 1898): 57.

Confederate Veteran. Note regarding to Lt. Robert Noland. 20 (June 1912): 272.

Confederate Veteran. Note regarding Captain Edward S. Parker. 23 (January 1915): 41.

Confederate Veteran. Note regarding Richard Seckel. 28 (April 1920): 148.

Confederate Veteran. "Capture of the Maple Leaf." Note pertaining to John B. Wolf. 6 (August 1898): 386.

Cornish, Dudley Taylor. *The Sable Arm - Black Troops in the Union Army, 1961-1965.* Lawrence, Kans.: University Press of Kansas, 1987.

Creecy, Richard Benbury. *Grandfather's Tales of North Carolina History.* Raleigh: Edwards & Broughton, Printers, 1901.

Crute, Joseph H., Jr. *Units of the Confederate States Army.* Midlothian, Va.: Derwent Books, 1987.

Downer, Edward T. "Johnson's Island." *Civil War History* 8 (June 1962): 202-217.

Edmonds, David C. *The Guns of Port Hudson.* Vol. 2, *The Investment, Siege and Reduction.* Lafayette, La.: The Arcadia Press, 1984.

Evans, Clement, ed. *Confederate Military History.* vol. 2, *Maryland,* by Bradley T. Johnson; vol. 5, *North Carolina,* by D. H. Hill, Jr.; vol. 8, *Alabama,* by Joseph Wheeler; vol. 10, *Arkansas,* by John M Harrell; vol. 11, *Kentucky,* by J. Stoddard Johnston; vol. 13, by *Louisiana,* by John Dimitry; vol. 15, *Texas,* by O. M. Roberts. Atlanta: Confederate

Publishing Co., 1899; repr., Wilmington, NC: Broadfoot Publishing Co., 1988.

Freeman, Douglas Southall. *The South to Posterity*. New York: Charles Scribner's Sons, 1951.

Gibson, Thomas R. "Gen. James H. McBride." *Confederate Veteran* 23 (August 1915): 375.

Gladstone, William. "The Colonel's Messmate." *Civil War Times Illustrated*, September/October 1989.

Headquarters Heliogram (Newsletter of the Council on America's Military Past), August 1991.

Hesseltine, William Best. "Military Prisons of St. Louis, 1861-1865." *The Missouri Historical Review* 23 (April 1929): 380.

———. Introduction to "Civil War Prisons." *Civil War History* 8 (June 1962): 109-112.

———. *Civil War Prisons - A Study in War Psychology*. Columbus, Ohio: The Onio State University Press, 1930.

Heyl, Erik. *Early American Steamers*, vols. 1 and 5. Buffalo, N.Y.: Erik Heyl, 1967.

Holland, Keith V., Lee B. Manley, and James W. Towart. *The Maple Leaf - An Extraordinary American Civil War Shipwreck*. Jacksonville, Fla.: St Johns Archaeological Expeditions, Inc., 1993.

Hoehling, A. A. and Mary Hoehling. *The Last Days of the Confederacy*. New York: The Fairfax Press, 1981.

[Jones, Buehring H.]. *Memorial of the Federal Prison on Johnson's Island, Lake Erie, Ohio, 1862-1864*. Collections of the Virginia Historical Society, 1887.

LaBree, Ben. ed. *The Confederate Soldier in the Civil War: The Campaigns, Battles, Sieges, Charges and Skirmishes.* Patterson, N.J.: Pageant Books, 1959.

Lewis, Emanuel Raymond. *Seacoast Fortifications of the United States.* Washington, D.C.: Smithsonian Institution Press, 1970.

Lewis, George G, and John Mewha. *History of Prisoner of War Utilization by the United States Army 1776-1945.* U.S. Department of the Army Pamphlet 20-213. Washington, D.C.: GPO, 1955.

Long, E. B. and Barbara. *The Civil War Day By Day - An Almanac, 1861-1865.* Garden City, N.Y.: Doubleday, 1971.

Melchor, James. *Fort Norfolk.* Unpublished history of Fort Norfolk in files of author.

Melchor, Marilyn S. and Debbie Brooks. Transcript of graffiti found on walls at Fort Norfolk, August 1991, in files of author.

Miller, Francis T., ed. *The Photographic History of the Civil War.* Vol. 4, *Prisons and Hospitals* by Holland Thompson. New York: Review of Reviews, 1911.

Moore, Frank, ed. *The Rebellion Records, A Diary of American Events, with Documents, Narratives, Illustrative Incidents, Poetry, etc.* New York: Putnam, 1861-1871; repr. New York: Arno Press Inc., 1977. Vol. 7.

Morris, Gouverneur. *The History of a Volunteer Regiment - Being a Succinct Account of the Organization, Services, and Adventures of the Sixth Regiment New York Volunteer Infantry Known as Wilson's Zouaves.* New York: Veteran Volunteer Pub. Co., 1891.

Munden, Kenneth W. and Henry Putney Beers. *Guide to Federal Archives Relating to the Civil War*, National Archives Publication No 63-1. Washington, D.C.: GPO, 1962.

Myers, John Myers. *San Francisco's Reign of Terror*. Garden City, N.Y.: Doubleday & Company, 1966.

Oates, Stephen B. *The Fires of Jubilee: Nat Turner's Fierce Rebellion*. New York: Harper & Row, Publishers, 1975.

Parramore, Thomas C. "The Roanoke-Chowan Story," in *Civil War Stories*, *Ahoskie Daily Roanoke-Chowan News*, 1960.

Powell, William S. *The North Carolina Gazetter*. Chapel Hill, N.C.: University of North Carolina Press, 1968.

Pugh, Jesse Forbes. *Three Hundred Years Along the Pasquotank: A Biographical History of Camden County*. Old Trap, N.C.: Jesse Pugh, 1957.

Roberts, W. Adolph. *Semmes of the Alabama*. New York: The Bobbs-Merrill Company, 1938.

Royce, Josiah. *California*. Boston and New York: Houghton, Mifflin and Company, 1886, repr. New York: AMS Press Inc., 1973.

Scharf, J. Thomas. *History of the Confederate States Navy*. New York: Rogers & Sherwood, 1887.

Shannonhouse, Edna M., comp. and ed. *Yearbook*. Elizabeth City, N.C.: The Pasquotank Historical Society, 1983. Vol. 4.

Southern Historical Society Papers. "Thrilling Incident: Capture of the Federal Steamer Maple Leaf." 24 (January-December 1896): 165-71, quoting from the *Richmond Dispatch*, April 26, 1896.

Taylor, Joe Gray. *Louisiana Reconstructed, 1863-1877*. Baton Rouge: Louisiana State University Press, 1974.

Time Life Series, "The Civil War." *First Blood* and *Spies, Scouts and Raiders*. Alexandria, Va.: Time Life Books, 1985.

Watson, David A. *Perquimans County - A Brief History*. Raleigh: Division of Archives and History, Department of Cultural Resources, 1987.

Weinert, Richard P., Jr. *The Confederate Regular Army*. Shippensburg, Pa.: White Mane Publishing Company, 1991.

Weinert, Richard P., Jr., and Colonel Robert Arthur. *Defender of the Chesapeake - The Story of Fort Monroe*. Annapolis, Md.: Leeward Publications, Inc., 1978.

Whitten, J. G. Introduction to *My Life in Prison and Escape* by John Uriah Green. Navasota, Tex.: Navasota Examiner Review, 1952.

Wiley, Irvin Bell. *The Life of Johnny Reb - The Common Soldier of the Confederacy*. Baton Rouge and London: Louisiana State University Press, 1943.

Williams, Mary Floyd. *History of the San Francisco Committee of Vigilance of 1851*. Berkeley: University of California Press, 1921.

Wilson, Samuel, Jr. *A History of the U.S. Customhouse in New Orleans*. New Orleans: U.S. Custom Service, Region V, 1982.

Wilson, W. Emerson. *Fort Delaware*. Wilmington, Del.: Old Wilmington Printing Co., 1955; repr. William P. Frank, ed., Fort Delaware Historical Society, 1983.

Winthrop, William. *Military Law and Precedent*. Washington, D.C.: The Adjutant General, U.S. War Department, 1886; repr. GPO, 1920.

Works Progress Administration Federal Writers' Project. *Delaware, a Guide to the First State*. New York: Viking Press, 1938.

Works Progress Administration Federal Writers' Project. *New Orleans City Guide*. Boston: Houghton Mifflin Company, 1938.

Index

The index does not cover the list of illustrations or the the roster of prisoners held on the *Maple Leaf* (Appendix A)

130

www.ingramcontent.com/pod-product-compliance
Lightning Source LLC
Chambersburg PA
CBHW070450090426
42735CB00012B/2502